Power Verbs for

Jo   's

Power Verbs for Job Seekers

Hundreds of Verbs and Phrases to Bring Your Résumés, Cover Letters, and Job Interviews to Life

Michael Lawrence Faulkner
with Michelle Faulkner-Lunsford

Vice President, Publisher: Tim Moore
Associate Publisher and Director of Marketing: Amy Neidlinger
Executive Editor: Jeanne Glasser Levine
Editorial Assistant: Pamela Boland
Operations Specialist: Jodi Kemper
Marketing Manager: Megan Graue
Cover Designer: Chuti Prasertsith
Managing Editor: Kristy Hart
Project Editor: Anne Goebel
Copy Editor: Gill Editorial Services
Proofreader: Jess DeGabriele
Senior Indexer: Cheryl Lenser
Senior Compositor: Gloria Schurick
Manufacturing Buyer: Dan Uhrig

© 2013 by Michael Lawrence Faulkner
Publishing as FT Press
Upper Saddle River, New Jersey 07458

FT Press offers excellent discounts on this book when ordered in quantity for bulk purchases or special sales. For more information, please contact U.S. Corporate and Government Sales, 1-800-382-3419, corpsales@pearsontechgroup.com. For sales outside the U.S., please contact International Sales at international@pearsoned.com.

Company and product names mentioned herein are the trademarks or registered trademarks of their respective owners.

Printed in the United States of America

First Printing February 2013

ISBN-10: 0-13-315872-1
ISBN-13: 978-0-13-315872-4

Pearson Education LTD.
Pearson Education Australia PTY, Limited.
Pearson Education Singapore, Pte. Ltd.
Pearson Education Asia, Ltd.
Pearson Education Canada, Ltd.
Pearson Educación de Mexico, S.A. de C.V.
Pearson Education—Japan
Pearson Education Malaysia, Pte. Ltd.

Library of Congress Cataloging-in-Publication Data

Faulkner, Michael.
  Power verbs for job seekers : hundreds of verbs and phrases to bring
your résumés, cover letters, and job interviews to life / Michael
Faulkner. — 1 Edition.
      pages cm
  ISBN 978-0-13-315872-4 (pbk. : alk. paper)
  1. Résumés (Employment) 2. Cover letters. 3. Job hunting. 4.
English language—Verb. 5. English language—Verb phrase. I. Title.
  HF5383.F38 2013
  650.14—dc23
                                                          2012050097

Dedicated to Ken Boyer, the gatekeeper.

Ken was my first college professor and had a powerful influence on the direction of my life.

Table of Contents

Acknowledgments

There were many people who helped with this book in many ways. Much of this help was a family affair. My wife Jo-Ann lent her love, patience, support, and advice. My son Kenny provided ideas for format when I was at a dead end. My grandsons Andrew and Alex helped by looking up some words, and my daughter Michelle did yeoman's work: performing edits, writing content, working on style, and giving advice.

About the Authors

Dr. Michael Lawrence Faulkner is the author of six books. He is a Professor at the Keller Graduate School of Management at DeVry University. He is a former U.S. Marine, who spent 30 years in a variety of leadership and executive management positions with Fortune 500 firms and major nonprofit trade associations, as well as helping run the family business before beginning his second career in academics. Michael is a member of MENSA, a Rotary International Fellow, the Keller Master Teacher Award, and holds a Silver Certification by the Toastmaster's International. In addition to his Ph.D., Michael has earned two Master's degrees, one from NYU and an MBA from NYIT.

Michelle Faulkner-Lunsford is a 2001 graduate of Middle Tennessee State University, where she majored in English and minored in Writing. Mrs. Lunsford spent 10+ years in the world of advertising and marketing as an Account Manager and Director of Marketing and New Business Development, managing multi-million dollar accounts ranging from male enhancement medications to beer ads. In 2011, Michelle left the corporate world for the opportunity to raise her daughter.

CHAPTER 1

Why and How Power Verbs Can Pump Up Your Résumés, Cover Letters, Interviews, and Personal Networking Efforts

The power verbs in this book are those that can be used for job searching and networking. They are arranged alphabetically under major and minor categories of the most desirable and sought-after human values, personality traits, personal characteristics, behaviors, and employability skills. There has been substantial empirical research done on the topic of what employers are really looking for in applicants. The results of these studies—what employers really seek in job applicants—were used to provide the framework for what power verbs to include and how to best organize them for readers.

The authors have included hundreds of the most useful power verbs as part of the practical implicit approach to employers and networking contacts. Job searchers can pump up their résumés, cover letters, thank-you notes, interviews, and other forms of human communications that are critical to job searching. In addition, individuals who want to enhance their personal, social, and business lives by building a powerful network can enhance their networking skills.

HOW TO USE THIS BOOK

Those of you searching for attention-grabbing, highly impactful power verbs should think about the kinds of critical employability skills and the most desirable employability and personality skills by broad topics (for example: accomplishments and achievements, communication skills, ability to work with teams, and ability to find and fix problems). Once you've determined these broad categories of skills and traits, you can search alphabetically to refine the hunt for just the right power verbs. To help you find all possible power verbs, cross-check words in the index.

The power verbs that are not in common use have international pronunciation included.

Each power verb has synonyms and abbreviated definitions to help you position just the right power verbs for the impact and effect you desire.

In most cases, the power verbs include examples of the specific word in actual use as a "Résumé bullet point." Bulleted points have a style purpose that says, "Something important follows." Employment experts have recognized for some time that smartly bulleted résumé points are the most effective, efficient, and productive method for job seekers to display their value to a prospective employer. The problem is that good people have had exciting, responsible jobs and have accomplished significant achievements in their work and social lives, but fail to correctly display these achievements in bullet form. While many employ the bullet model, they have two fundamental but deadly flaws. First, résumés frequently include too many bullet points. Second, many of the bullets included were somewhat dull narrations repeating, in synonyms, job descriptions that have already been indicated.

Résumé bullet points should draw attention to your accomplishments—your quantitative selling points. Résumé bullet points depict achievements and should not just restate the job description. An achievement is anything that can be measured in numbers, dollars, percentages, or some measure showing improvement due to some action, attainment, decision, deed, endeavor, exploit, feat, step, success, undertaking, venture, or work attributed to you.

Hiring managers are busy people and appreciate applicants who respect their time by providing a few (3 to 4) simple, easy-to-read, yet impactful bullets of their achievements for each position. Note that we said achievements; we did not say restatements of their job description. Your résumé is a form of an extended calling card, and its purpose is to get you a face-to-face interview, not tell your entire working history.

Some power verbs include a field titled "Collocates to." This is a listing of primarily less familiar words that includes other terms that have a tendency to be grouped or chunked together with that verb.

Some power verbs include the power verb that is used in a sentence, a quotation, a newspaper article, or a magazine article.

How to Find the Right Power Verb

Soft skills are listed in Chapter 3: the critical employability skills, behaviors, and personality traits that employers are looking for in job seekers.

Hard skills are listed in Chapter 4: those personal skills and experiences that employers say are of equal importance to employability skills.

Experience, credentials, and education are listed in Chapter 5: achievements and accomplishments likely to be of importance to employers.

Many power verbs can be used in multiple categories. When a power verb can be employed in a crossover category, this is shown next to the power verb.

Every employer looks for a specific set of skills from job seekers that match the skills necessary to perform a particular job. But beyond these job-specific technical skills, certain skills are nearly universally sought by employers. The good news is that most job seekers possess these skills to some extent. The better news is that job seekers who have weaknesses in these areas can improve their skills through training, professional development, or obtaining coaching/mentoring from someone who understands these skills.

The best news is that once you understand the skills and characteristics that most employers seek, you can tailor your job-search communication— your résumé, cover letter, and interview language—to showcase how well your background aligns with common employer requirements.

Numerous studies have identified these critical employability skills, sometimes referred to as "soft skills." We've distilled the skills from these many studies into this list of skills most frequently mentioned. Look for ways to include, inject, weave, identify, and show examples of these characteristics in your résumé, cover letters, and answers to interview questions.

Now, go search for the power verbs that will pump up your job searching and networking!

CHAPTER 2

Soft Skills Related to Professional Capabilities: Performance and Grooming

ACCOUNTABILITY

Accountability is the recognition, acknowledgment, and assumption of personal responsibility for one's actions, such as decisions and polices. It includes the obligation to report, explain, and be answerable for resulting consequences.

ABET

{also use in Commitment and Dedication, Learn, Motivated, and Social Intelligence}

(1) advocate; approve; assist; back; back up; encourage; espouse; foment; help incite; put up to; sanction; support; urge (especially in wrongdoing)

(1) Abetted by high oil prices, Exxon announced that its profits had tripled.

Collocates to: aided, decisions, enemies, people, progress, trends

Résumé bullet points:

• Abetted the decision to expand globally

ABIDE

{also use in Common Sense, Commitment and Dedication, Cross-Cultural Competency, Professional Demeanor and Presence, Reliability, Self-Manageable, and Work Ethic}

(1) bear; continue; endure; go on being; put up with; stomach; take; tolerate

(1) Abided by a set of loose restrictions, I formed and started the business on very little capital.

(2)   hold; remain; stay; stand fast; stand for

Collocates to: agreements, conditions, laws, norms, rules; resolutions, wishes

Résumé bullet points:

  • Abided by the vision of the founder and kept the US plant open

ABSORB

{also use in Accomplishments and Achievements, Cognitive Load Management, Common Sense, Commitment and Detail, Cross-Cultural Competency, Flexibility, Learn, and Self-Manageable}

(1)   acquire; assimilate; attract; consume; digest; endure; engulf; fascinate; imbibe; soak up; sustain; take in; use up

   (1) During the recent economic downturn, Boeing absorbed most of the price increases.

(2)   draw into oneself; grasp; realize; recognize; take in; understand

(3)   become captivated, interested, engaged or preoccupied in; fascinated

Collocates to: concepts, carbon, ideas, immigrants, liquids, solar, sunlight

Résumé bullet points:

  • Absorbed myself in all new responsibilities

ACCEDE

{also use in Commitment and Dedication, Customer Awareness, Flexibility, Outgoing, and Social Intelligence}

(1)   agree; allow; approach; ascend; attain; come to; comply; conform; consent; enter upon; give assent; grant; succeed to; take over

   (1) The unions acceded to the pension rule changes.

Collocates to demands, needs, new ideas, requests

Résumé bullet points:

  • Acceded to subordinates significantly higher levels of authority and responsibility, thus improving morale and productivity

ACCENTUATE

{also use in Accuracy and Preciseness, Attention to Detail, Cognitive Load Management, Commitment and Dedication, Communication, Creativity, Drive and Passion, Leadership, and Motivated}

(1)   accent; emphasize; heighten; intensify

(2)   make more noticeable; play up; stress something

(1), (2) The recession <u>accentuated</u> the negative feelings many stock-holders had about wasteful spending.

<u>Collocates to: differences, opportunities, positives, shapes</u>

Résumé bullet points:

- <u>Accentuated</u> company's strategic objectives in the design and writing of annual report, which won an award from the PR Association

ACCEPT

{also use in Cross-Cultural Competency, Reliability, Take Direction, and Team Player}

(1)   admit; agree; believe; consent; say you will

(2)   receive with gladness and approval

(3)   take something being offered

(4)   bow to; endure; put up with; resign yourself to; tolerate

Résumé bullet points:

- <u>Accepted</u> into the industry's certification committee in only my seventh year in the business, which impacted the field

ACCOMPLISH

{also use in Accomplishments and Achievements, Accuracy and Precision, Attention to Detail, Drive, Passion and Tenacity, Leadership, Motivated, Novel and Adaptive Thinking, and Work Ethic}

(1)   achieve; attain; bring about; carry out; cause to happen; complete; do; gain; get done; finish; fulfill; make happen; make possible; produce; pull off; reach; realize; undertake

<u>Collocates to: goals, job, mission, objectives strategy, tactics, task, work</u>

Résumé bullet points:

- <u>Accomplished</u> all major objectives of firm's highly touted HR program, "The Extra Mile"

- <u>Accomplished</u> all new project objectives of a major plant relocation, coming in 10 percent under budget, two months ahead of schedule, and without any loss of productivity

ACCREDIT

{also use in Attention to Detail, Customer Awareness, Reliability, and HARD SKILLS: Administration and Organizational}

(1)   approve; attribute; authorize; credit to; endorse; recognize; sanction

(2)   certify; supply with credentials or authority
Collocates to: councils, hospitals, institutions, investors, programs, schools, training

Résumé bullet points:

 • Accredited by the Promotion Marketing Association in 2012

ACKNOWLEDGE

{also use in Honesty, Integrity, Learn, Outgoing, Professional Demeanor, and Self-Manageable}

(1)   admit; allow; avow; concede; confess; fess up; grant; own up; recognize

(2)   answer; react; reply; respond; return

(3)   greet; nod to; salute; wave to
Collocates to: existence, contribution, fact, failure issue, need, problem, reality, support

Résumé bullet points:

 • Acknowledged by industry association as one of the field's Top 50
   thought leaders

ACQUIESCE

{also use in Attitude, Cognitive Load Management, Compassion, and Social Intelligence}

(1)   accept; agree; assent; consent; comply with passively; concur; concede; consent; give in; go along with; submit; yield

 (1) The union acquiesced, and the company switched pension plan from a defined benefit to a 401(k) plan, saving hundreds of millions of dollars in future benefit liabilities.

Résumé bullet points:

 • Acquiesced to consumer input and led firm's redesign and remarketing of
   digital action hero toy, keeping a multimillion dollar revenue stream alive

ADDUCE

(1)   allege; bring forward; cite as evidence; lead to; present; put forward

 (1) Jorge adduced that the product's failure was due to poor engineering..

Résumé bullet points:

 • Adduced the main reasons for the firm's drop in market share for the
   Board of Directors, providing direction for the strategic planning
   committee

ADJUDICATE

{also use in Cognitive Load Management, Critical Thinking and Design Mind-Set}

(1)   act as judge; listen; mediate; preside over argument; settle

> *(1) The Labor Relations Board <u>adjudicated</u> the dismissed employee's case.*

<u>Collocates to: cases, disputes, infractions, nexus, quarrels</u>

Résumé bullet points:

- <u>Adjudicated</u> disputes between nonunion workers, improving worker morale and productivity

ADJUST

{also use in Common Sense, Cross-Cultural Competency, Engineering, Flexibility, R&D, and Work Ethic}

(1)   accommodate; alter; amend; attune; bend; change; correct; fine-tune; fix; modify; pacify; rectify; regulate; resolve; settle; tune up; tweak

<u>Collocates to: compensate, ideas, models, standards, themes, work</u>

Résumé bullet points:

- <u>Adjusted</u> all company revenues projections using the NPV model, producing a more accurate determination of actual needs and reducing the money borrowed by 20 percent

ADMINISTER

{also use in Reliability, Self-Manageable, HARD SKILLS: Accounting and Finance, and Administrative, Organizational, Planning and Time Management}

(1)   control; deal out; direct; dispense; furnish a benefit; give out; govern; hand out; manage; mete out; order; run; supervise; oversee a process

> *(1) Surveys <u>administered</u> after the customer focus groups showed a high level of satisfaction.*

<u>Collocates to: contracts, exams, plans, polices, programs, projects, tests</u>

Résumé bullet points:

- <u>Administered</u> the first in-house "English as a second language" training program assisting hundreds of immigrant workers in learning English faster

ADOPT

{also use in Accomplishments and Achievements and Commitment and Dedication}

(1)   accept; agree to; assume; approve; choose; embrace; endorse; espouse; foster; implement; take in as one's own; take on; take up; take on board
Collocates to: approaches, concepts, ideas, plans, policies, procedures, processes, regulations, resolutions, rules, standards, strategies, systems, tactics
Résumé bullet points:

- Adopted new work rules, which provided greater efficiency and improved productivity, thus lowering production costs

AFFIRM

{also use in Attention to Detail and Accuracy, Critical Thinking and Problem Solving, and Honesty and Integrity}

(1)   acknowledge; affirm; announce; assert; asseverate; avow; confirm; establish; insist; pronounce; state; validate; verify

(2)   encourage; sustain; support; uphold
Collocates to: beliefs, commitments, conviction, faith, importance, rights, rulings, strategy, values
Résumé bullet points:

- Affirmed the rights of our customers to return items without receipts, thus improving customer satisfaction as reported on monthly surveys

AGREE

{also use in Flexibility and Polite}

(1)   accord; affirm; concur; consent; get together; grant; harmonize; jibe; match; say yes; square
Résumé bullet points:

- Agreed to serve as a mentor for new hires, helping speed up learning curve

AID

(1)   abet; alleviate; assist; benefit; facilitate; give support to; help; minister to; serve; sustain; subsidize
Résumé bullet points:

- Aided new hires in understanding the nuances of a highly regulated business, reducing possibility of costly errors

ALTER

(1)   adjust; amend; castrate; change; correct; covert; modify; revise; rework; vary

(1) I <u>altered</u> the Product Innovation Charter to include the goals we had set for the new product.

Résumé bullet points:

- <u>Altered</u> long-standing misconceptions regarding the acceptance of commercial mail, enabling a refocus on medium and growth of sales by 40 percent

AMELIORATE

{also use in Accomplishments and Achievements, Accuracy and Preciseness, Attention to Detail, Creativity, Leadership, Novel and Adaptive Thinking, and Self-Manageable}

(1)   correct a mistake; improve; make better; tolerate

(2)   correct a deficiency or defect; make right a wrong; take action that makes up for one's negative or improper actions

(1), (2) The antiquated inventory system must be <u>ameliorated</u>.

<u>Collocates to: difficulties, problems, shortcomings</u>

Résumé bullet points:

- <u>Ameliorated</u> the firm's prior disposal procedures and gained wide acceptance by consumer groups

APPOINT

(1)   assign; delegate; determine; design; designate; employ; make; take on

Résumé bullet points:

- <u>Appointed</u> as first nondirector to organization's strategic planning committee, adding diversity to decision making
- <u>Appointed</u> to liaison with global investor groups

APPROVE

{also use in Design Mind-Set and Self-Manageable}

(1)   accept; agree to; attest; back up; command; commend; endorse; favor; praise; ratify; sanction; support

(1) Of the five new company products <u>approved</u> by the FDA, four were done by project management teams that I managed.

(2)   allow; authorize; consent; grant; pass; sanction

Collocates to: budgets, deals, plans, ideas, new policies and procedures, requests

Résumé bullet points:

> • Approved the requests for continuing education assistance

ARRANGE

{also use in Creativity and HARD SKILLS: Administrative and Organizational}

(1)   array; authorize; catalogue; classify; fix; order; organize; position; set up, sort

(2)   make plans for something to be done

Collocates to: alphabetically, ascending, carefully, chronologically, descending, haphazardly, hierarchically, symmetrically

Résumé bullet points:

> • Arranged the company's workspace to include shared offices and resources, resulting in improvements of 20 percent productivity

ASCERTAIN

{also use in Accuracy and Preciseness}

(1)   determine; discover; establish; find out; learn; realize; uncover

(2)   find out with certainty

Résumé bullet points:

> • Ascertained that the firm's international vendors were adding discretionary fees in favorable currencies to them, which increased our annual costs by 8 percent

ASCRIBE

{also use in Accuracy and Preciseness, Attention to Detail, Computational Thinking, and Honesty and Integrity}

(1)   accredit; arrogate; assert that something has been caused by someone or something; attribute something to someone

Collates to: ideas, meaning, powers, tendencies, traits, values

Résumé bullet points:

> • Ascribed the differences in speed to completion and subsequent cost savings to prototyping

ASSIGN

{also use in Accuracy and Preciseness, Computational Thinking, and HARD SKILLS: Administrative and Operational}

(1) allocate; allot; choose; consign; dispense; dole out; give; hand over; pick; select; transfer

(2) appoint; delegate; designate; detail; name

Résumé bullet points:

* Assigned to the organization's new product development committee

AUTHENTICATE

{also use in Accuracy and Preciseness}

(1) confirm; endorse; serve to prove; substantiate; validate

Résumé bullet points:

* Authenticated the proof of consumer claims on main product line, reducing potential costs of overpayment by $2 million

AUTHORIZE

(1) accredit; commission; empower; enable; entitle; license; grant; qualify

Résumé bullet points:

* Authorized all department purchases, totaling $13 million in 2012

BALANCE

{also use in Attention to Detail, Critical Thinking and Problem Solving, and Cross-Cultural Competency}

(1) assess; calculate; collate; compare; consider; evaluate; even out; equalize; keep upright; offset; settle; square; stabilize; stay poised; steady; tally; total; weigh; weight up

Collocates to: amendments, approach, budgets, life plan, view

Résumé bullet points:

* Balanced the organization's budget five consecutive years, thus creating incentive for improved donations

BEGIN

(1) get underway; start

(2) actuate; arise; commence; come into being; generate; inaugurate; initiate; originate; usher in

(3)   have a first part
Collocates to: carriers, holidays plans, studies, journeys

Résumé bullet points:

- Began all the sales meetings with motivational stories of individual success

BLUE PENCIL

(1)   censor; correct or edit writing, as if by changing or deleting; cross out

   (1) I blue penciled the business plan submitted by the consultant.

BUILD

{also use in Customer Awareness and Engineering and R&D}

(1)   construct; erect; put up; raise; rear

(2)   grow; improve; increase

Résumé bullet points:

- Built the company's very first production prototype by employing 3D printing technology
- Built new business from start-to profitability in 19 months

CALCULATE

{also use in Accounting and Finance, Computational Thinking, and Engineering and R&D}

(1)   account; coax; compute; consider; deem; determine something; entice; enumerate; figure; persuade

Résumé bullet points:

- Calculated the firm's annual cost of technology, allowing for more accurate annual budgeting

CATALOG

(1)   arrange; classify; list; put together; register

Résumé bullet points:

- Cataloged the 50-year history of customer suggestions into a searchable database of product improvement opportunities

CHAIR

(1)   be in charge; manage; oversee committee or function
Résumé bullet points:

- Chaired the firm's investment committee that picked an investment portfolio that outperformed the DOW by 10 percent

CHAMPION

{also use in Commitment and Dedication, Leadership, Novel and Adaptive
Thinking, and Self-Confidence}

(1)   advocate; back; be a winner; campaign for; crusade for; excel; fight for;
stand up for; support; uphold
Collocates to: approaches, causes, freedom, ideas, issues, reforms, values
Résumé bullet points:

- Championed the concept for an in-house day care center

COALESCE

{also use in Accomplishments and Achievements, Cognitive Load
Management, Commitment and Dedication, Cross-Cultural Competency,
Flexibility, Leadership, Learn, Social Intelligence, and Team Player}

(1)   come together as one; combine; grow together; join; unite
Résumé bullet points:

- Coalesced more than 100 diverse stakeholders into an effective, efficient
company asset

COMPLETE

{also use in Accomplishments and Achievements, Commitment and
Dedication, Education, Self-Manageable, and Work Ethic}

(1)   choate; complete; conclude; be done; entire; finish a task intact; integral;
perfect; through; unabridged; uncut; whole; wrap up
Résumé bullet points:

- Completed all requirements for 2012 annual evaluation by the second
quarter

CONCEIVE

{also use in Accomplishments and Achievements, Critical Thinking and
Problem Solving, and Self-Manageable}

(1)   create; envisage; imagine; invent original idea; picture; visualize

(2)   begin life; dream; elaborate; form; make up

Résumé bullet points:

- Conceived the firm's first social media strategy that extended the brand globally

CONSTRUE

(1)   analyze something in a certain way; explain; infer or deduce; interpret; translate

(1) Exuding confidence and showing enthusiasm are often *construed* *as signs of high intelligence.*

DEFINE

{also use in Accomplishments and Achievements, Accuracy and Preciseness, Attention to Detail, Critical Thinking and Problem Solving, Design Mind-Set}

(1)   characterize; classify; describe; determine or set down boundaries; distinguish; identify; label; term

(2)   circumscribe; delimitate; delimit; demarcate; mark out

Résumé bullet points:

- Defined the priorities for the board's strategic planning committee

DELINEATE

{also use in Attention to Detail, Communication, and HARD SKILLS: Analytical, Research, Computational}

(1)   describe accurately; determine; draw an outline; fix boundaries; identify or indicate by marking with precision; represent something

Collocates to: areas, boundaries, differences, factors, structure

Résumé bullet points:

- Delineated the scope of internal audits for the division, making them more efficient and effective

DEPICT

{also use in Cognitive Load Management and Communications}

(1)   describe; get a picture of; give a picture of; illustrate; picture in words; portray; present a lifelike image; represent; show

Résumé bullet points:

- Depicted the surging top competitor as a wannabe and thus lifted the sales team morale so they could redouble their efforts

DESIGNATE

(1)   call; circumscribe; choose; elect; entitle; identify; label; name; nominate; select; style; title

(2)   allocate; indicate; point out; specify

Résumé bullet points:

- <u>Designated</u> the locations for the firm's annual franchise television advertising promotion

EARMARK

{also use in Accuracy and Preciseness, Attention to Detail, Commitment and Dedication, and Time Management}

(1)   allocate; allot; appropriate; assign; reserve for special purpose; set aside

(2)   mark the ears of livestock for special identification

(3)   set a distinctive mark on

<u>Collocates to: money, processes, spending</u>

Résumé bullet points:

- <u>Earmarked</u> the department's cost savings for individual bonuses

EDIT

{also use in Attention to Detail, Communication, and Take Direction}

(1)   alter; correct; revise and make ready

(2)   prepare a written work for publication by selection, arrangement, and annotation

(3)   make additions, deletions, or other changes

Résumé bullet points:

- <u>Edited</u> the company's customer newsletter, which was a tool that enhanced retention and improved renewal rates

ELUCIDATE

{also use in Cognitive Load Management, Communication, Social Intelligence, Take Direction, and HARD SKILLS: Analytical, Research, and Computational}

(1)   clarify; explain; make something clear; explicate; expose; expound; illuminate; lucid; reveal; throw light on it

   (1) The impact on the new pricing policy has not been fully <u>elucidated</u>.

EMPOWER

{also use in Drive, Passion, Tenacity, and Work Ethic}

(1) allow; authorize; give authority or power to; sanction

(2) make one stronger and more confident, especially in controlling his life and claiming his rights

(1), (2) Our shareholders came away from the annual meeting feeling more <u>empowered</u>.

Résumé bullet points:

- <u>Empowered</u> my customer service staff with authority and responsibility, improving department productivity by 20 percent

ENDORSE

(1) accept; agree; approve

(2) sign on the back of a check

(3) give sanction to an idea, plan, proposal, or candidate

(1) Our new product was <u>endorsed</u> by the largest consumer protection organization in the United States.

Résumé bullet points:

- <u>Endorsed</u> the employee benefits committee recommendation to include substance abuse in the employee medical benefit package

ENFORCE

(1) carry out; compel; execute; impose; insist; invoke

(2) give force to; urge

(3) bring about or impose by force; compel observance of
Résumé bullet points

- <u>Enforced</u> the department's ethics policies

ENSURE

{also use in Accuracy and Preciseness}

(1) follow; guarantee; make certain; make sure

(2) make safe; secure; protect
Résumé bullet points:

- <u>Ensured</u> all hiring managers complied with federal EEOC regulations

- <u>Ensured</u> the accuracy and completeness of field training manuals

ENUMERATE

(1)   catalog; count off; itemize; list; tally

(2)   determine the number of; total

(3)   name one by one; specify

Résumé bullet points:

- Enumerated the benefits of expanding operations globally to the Board of Directors

ESPOUSE

(1)   adopt; advocate; back; champion; promote; support; take up

Résumé bullet points:

- Espoused zero tolerance for digital bullying

ESTABLISH

{also use in Accomplishments and Achievements, Reliability, and Self-Confidence}

(1)   begin; create; enact; ensconce; found; install; institute; prove; set up; settle; start

(2)   make firm; make stable

(3)   bring about; cause to happen

(4)   settle in an office or position

(5)   cause to accept or recognize; set up permanently

(6)   demonstrate; prove

Résumé bullet points:

- Established the first social media center for the company, providing a unified center for social media policy

- Established software simulation and modeling methods to assist marketing in determining that a customer's "voice" procedure is now standard operating procedure (SOP)

EXCEED

{also use in Accomplishments and Achievements}

(1)   beat; go beyond; be more or greater than; outdo; surpass what was expected or thought possible

Résumé bullet points

- Exceeded the firm's record for retaining existing customers by 50 percent, helping to achieve record profits for the firm

FORGE

(1)   come up with something

(2)   move ahead steadily

(3)   counterfeit; copy; falsify; fake

(4)   build; create; fashion; form

Résumé bullet points:

- Forged the first joint venture with the firm's vendors and our manufacturing operations

- Forged alliances with customer advocacy groups to create the industries' best record for service for six consecutive years (2006–2012)

FORMULATE

(1)   articulate; contrive; create; develop; devise; draft; elaborate; express; frame; put into words or expressions; invent; make; originate; plan; prepare; verbalize; voice

Résumé bullet points:

- Formulated a new multichannel marketing strategy that delivered a 40 percent increase in profits in the first year

- Formulated the firm's mission and vision statements, helping to solidify the brand

FULFILL

{also use in Accomplishments and Achievements and Reliability}

(1)   carry out; complete an assignment; discharge; execute; exercise; implement; perform; satisfy

Résumé bullet points:

- Fulfilled all requirements for industry's top certification in shortest time by any employee

GATHER

(1)   accumulate; assemble; collect; come together; garner; group; harvest

(2)   draw a conclusion

Résumé bullet points:

- Gathered the daily cash register receipts, floor manger notes, and customer suggestions and created a custom activity report for store manager

GENERATE

(1)   begat; breed; bring into being; cause; create; develop; engender; hatch;
      induce; make; produce; provoke; spawn; stir; touch off

Résumé bullet points:

- Generated a 30 percent increase in sales in first year of the new position

- Generated $15 million annual savings by revamping and accelerating
  productivity growth by developing more private branding

GIN UP

{also use in Common Sense and Self-Confidence}

(1)   create; encourage; produce; increase

*(1)   We were <u>ginned up</u> about the positive reviews of the new product
tests.*

GUIDE

(1)   conduct; channel; direct; funnel; point

(2)   escort; lead; pilot; route; surround; show; steer; supervise; usher

Résumé bullet points:

- Guided the firm's successful winning application for the 2012 National
  Productivity Award

HANDLE

{also use in Self-Manageable, and HARD SKILLS: Administrative and
Organizational}

(1)   carry out; come to grips with; conduct; control; cope with; deal with; have
      overall influence; hold responsible; manage; manipulate; ply; process;
      run; see to; sort out; supervise; undertake; wield

(2)   feel; finger; hold; manage with the hands; touch

Résumé bullet points:

- Handled all social and civic relationships for the firm creating a win-win
  situation for the community and the firm

- Handled all competitive SWOT analysis and strategic planning for a
  product line that represented $49 million, or 20 percent of total sales

IMPLEMENT

{also use in Accomplishments and Achievements and HARD SKILLS: Administrative and Organizational}

(1) accomplish; apply; carry out; complete; effect; employ; enforce; execute; fulfill; finish; instigate; put into action; put into operation; put into place; use; put into practice; put into service; realize

Collocates to: education, programs, regulations, rules, training, styles, transactions

Résumé bullet points:

- Implemented a social media strategy that gave the company an opportunity to join in the public conversation about outsourcing and thereby help shape the public opinion

- Implemented the firm's diversity recruiting and hiring plan that resulted in a more richly diverse pool of workers

IMPOSE

(1) apply or establish authority exact; assess; force one's self; levy; pass off; put

(1) "America has its origins in a rebellion against arbitrary and pernicious taxation and the framers wanted to make it extremely difficult to impose or raise taxes."

—David Gelernter, *Wall Street Journal*, Opinion, 07/02/2012

Résumé bullet points:

- Imposed work rules and merit bonuses on underperforming business units

IMPROVE

{also use in Accomplishments and Achievements, and Research and R&D}

(1) ameliorate; amend; better; build up; develop; employ; enhance in value; enrich; expand; further; help; get better; increase; make better; meliorate; perfect; raise to a better quality; upgrade use

(2) convalesce; get better; get stronger; get well; make progress; mend; perk up; rally; recover

Collocates to: abilities, efficiency, output, performance, profits, quality, results, sales, skills, timing

Résumé bullet points:

- Improved retention rates by 20 percent and improved the firm's profits by 8 percent

- Improved production output of new-to-the-world products by 15 percent by employing CAD technology

IMPUTE

{also use in Accuracy and Preciseness}

(1)   accredit; ascribe a result or quality to anything or anyone; assign; attribute; fix

(1) The database of prospects from this zip code imputed certain economic demographic characteristics.

(2)   accuse; allege; assert; challenge; charge; cite; implicate

Collocates to: datasets, omniscience, sanctification

INCREASE

{also use in Team Player}

(1)   add to; amplify; augment; boost; enhance; enlarge; improve; multiply; raise; swell

(2)   encourage; foster; fuel; intensify; redouble; strengthen

(3)   escalate; expand; grow; multiply; mushroom; proliferate; rise; soar; spread; swell

Résumé bullet points:

- Increased department's share of firm's profit from 20 percent to 40 percent in three years

- Increased the number of turn-key vendor relationships, which improved our just-in-time inventory operation and saved the firm $1million a year in downtime and labor costs

INFUSE

{also use in Creativity)

(1)   imbue; inculcate; ingrain; inspire; instill; introduce

(2)   teach a body of knowledge or perspective

(2) My extensive teaching skills along with my management approach infused a more enthusiastic outlook of the hourly workers and lead to a 22 percent reduction in missed days.

(3)   fill; permeate; pervade; suffuse

Résumé bullet points:

> • <u>Infused</u> a sense of pride and self-respect into a demoralized sales team; in one year, they won the national sales contest

INSTITUTE

(1)   found; get established; inaugurate; introduce; originate; set original activity in motion; set up; start

Résumé bullet points:

> • <u>Instituted</u> the firm's first diversity awareness training program, helping to reduce discrimination claims by 25 percent

> • <u>Instituted</u> a global cross-functional team culture that provided a foundation for quicker, more efficient, and more profitable product launches

INTERPOSE

{also use in Drive, Passion, and Tenacity}

(1)   arbitrate; be aggressive; insert; intercept; interfere; intermediate; meddle; mediate; offer assistance or presence; offer unsolicited opinion; put between

<u>Collocates to: arbitration, between, intermediation, mediation, rules</u>

Résumé bullet points:

> • <u>Interposed</u> an additional barrier between the host and the clients

INVIGORATE

(1)   animate; energize; enliven; galvanize; increase; liven; refresh; revitalize; strengthen; stimulate

> *(1) The older, more dispirited employees were the ones most <u>invigorated</u> by the message of the new president.*

Résumé bullet points:

> • <u>Invigorated</u> the organization's diversity outreach with a series of lectures, offsite visits, and cooperative ventures with diversity-owned businesses

LAUD

{also use in Communications, Outgoing, and Team Player}

(1)   acclaim; applaud; celebrate; extol; mention; praise; speak well of

> *(1) The sales team should be <u>lauded</u> for its new sales record.*

Collocates to: critics, efforts, ideas, plans, officials, leaders, others, vision, work

Résumé bullet points:

- Lauded by the media for innovative approaches to customer safety initiatives

LEVERAGE

(1)   control; force; influence; power; pull; weight

Résumé bullet points:

- Leveraged the product portfolio to enable the firm to maximize its 2012 sales

- Leveraged the diverse skills and abilities of the intradepartmental project management team and managed a blockbuster new product that exceeded revenues of all previous new products by 50 percent

MAXIMIZE

{also use in Accomplishments and Achievements, Accounting and Finance, and Drive, Passion, and Tenacity}

(1)   make as great or as large as possible; make best use of; raise to the highest possible degree

Résumé bullet points:

- Maximized the resource allocation so that department achieved record sales while trimming costs by 20 percent

- Maximized the advertising budget by more careful selection of target media, thus increasing revenues by 10 percent while holding cost to prior year

MEDIATE

(1)   arbitrate; act as a go-between; help settle difference of opinion; intercede; intervene; judge; reconcile; referee; umpire

Résumé bullet points:

- Mediated the dispute between fair hours for the 100 full-time staff and 200 part-time workers

MELIORATE

(1)   improve; make something better

(1) My work meliorated an already sound and effective strategy.

MILITATE

(1)   have a substantial effect on; weigh heavily on

     (1) My training manual <u>militated</u> our effort to get the new reps productive sooner.

NAIL DOWN

(1)   make certain; make sure; settle

     (1) I <u>nailed down</u> the labor contract in record time.

ORCHESTRATE

{also use in Attention to Detail and Design Mind-Set}

(1)   combine and adapt to obtain a particular outcome

(2)   arrange or organize surreptitiously to achieve a desired effect
Résumé bullet points:

     • <u>Orchestrated</u> the firm's sales growth that allowed it to achieve industry leadership

     • <u>Orchestrated</u> the firm's successful entry into global markets

ORIGINATE

(1)   bring into being; create or initiate; have a specified beginning; initiate; invent; make; start off

(2)   begin; come from; derive; start; stem from
Résumé bullet points:

     • <u>Originated</u> the advertising concept "Make a Need a Reality," the most successful ad campaign in the firm's history

OUTPERFORM

(1)   beat, better, exceed, or defeat
Résumé bullet points:

     • <u>Outperformed</u> 400 salespersons in the 2012 national sales contest

OVERSEE

{also use in HARD SKILLS: Administrative and Organizational, and Business and Business Sense}

(1)   administer; control; direct; keep an eye on; manage; run; supervise

Résumé bullet points:

- <u>Oversaw</u> the mergers and acquisition activities, which added $5 million to the bottom line

PERFORM

(1)   carry out; accomplish; fulfill an action; meet the requirements, task, or function; work; function or do something to a specified standard

(2)   present entertainment to an audience
Résumé bullet points:

- <u>Performed</u> as marketing liaison for clients of agency, providing added value

- <u>Performed</u> client interviews, researched information, and drafted affidavits, briefs, and contracts

POSIT

{also use in Attention to Detail and Critical Thinking and Problem Solving, and HARD SKILLS: Analytical, Research, and Computational}

(1)   assume; conceive; conjecture; hypothesize; imagine; postulate; put forward; speculate; suggest; state or assume as fact; theorize
<u>Collocates to: beliefs, concepts, idea, models, relationships, studies, theories</u>

PRECIPITATE

(1)   cause to happen abruptly or expectedly prematurely

(1) A boycott of the firm's products <u>precipitated</u> rigorous cost-cutting measures.

PREEMPT

(1)   seize something by prior right; take action in advance of another act to prevent that act
<u>Collocates to: laws, policies, procedures, programs, regulations, rules, schedules</u>

Résumé bullet points:

- <u>Preempted</u> what would have been expensive and punitive action by the FTC by writing self-regulatory practices that the industry adopted

RATIONALIZE

(1)   excuse; explain the action of

(1) The CEO <u>rationalized</u> the staff reductions by describing the corporation's value to customers.

(2)   interpret on the basis of some explainable reason

(3)   make actions conform to reason

RECTIFY

{also use in Accomplishments and Achievements and HARD SKILLS: Accounting and Finance}

(1)   amend; correct; fix; put right; resolve; set right

(2)   adjust; cure; mend; remedy; repair

(3)   convert

Résumé bullet points:

- <u>Rectified</u> long-standing imbalance between some sales territories and quotes, providing a more realistic policy and giving salespeople more incentive

SANCTION

{also use in Accuracy and Preciseness}

(1)   abet; authorize; confirm; countenance; give official permission; ratify; permit

(2)   impose penalty

(2) The Federal Communications Commission <u>sanctioned</u> the firm for violations of the Do Not Call rule.

SHOULDER

{also use in Professional Demeanor}

(1)   push along or through, with, or the shoulder

(2)   take or carry upon the shoulder

(3)   assume the burden of

<u>Collocates to: broad, burden, heavy, responsibilities, tall</u>

Résumé bullet points:

- <u>Shouldered</u> the responsibilities of two senior-level programmers for 18 months and maintained the department's commitment to its customers not to miss a single deadline

TRANSFORM

(1)   change from one form to another; remake; renew; upgrade

(2)   change the personality or character of one

(3)   change the condition, nature, or function of

Résumé bullet points:

> • Transformed an outdated, unproductive fulfillment center into the indus-
> try's leading center in 20 months

ACCURACY AND PRECISENESS

Accuracy and preciseness means being free from error or defect; consistent
with a standard, rule, or model; precise; exact; being careful or meticulous.

ABSTERGE

{also use in Accountability, Commitment and Dedication, Common Sense,
Customer Awareness, and Self-Manageable}

(1)   clean; cleanse; purge; wipe away

> *(1) One good quarterly report has not absterged the concern of investors.*

ACCENTUATE

{also use in Accountability, Attention to Detail, Cognitive Load Management,
Commitment and Dedication, Communication, Creativity, Drive and Passion,
Leadership, and Motivated}

(1)   accent; emphasize; heighten; intensify

> *(1) My branding plan accentuated the product's unique benefits in a way
> that more people could relate.*

(2)   make more noticeable; play up; stress something

Collocates to: differences, opportunities, positives, shapes

Résumé bullet points:

> • Accentuated company's technological leadership in the application for
> the Five Star Award

ACCOMPLISH

{also use in Accomplishments and Achievements, Accountability, Attention to
Detail, Drive, Leadership, Motivated, Novel and Adaptive Thinking, Passion
and Tenacity, and Work Ethic}

(1)   achieve; attain; bring about; carry out; cause to happen; complete; do;
      gain; get done; finish; fulfill; make happen; make possible; produce; pull
      off; reach; realize; undertake

Résumé bullet points:

- • <u>Accomplished</u> the five-year logistics reorganization plan in four years,
  saving $300,000 in investment costs

- • <u>Accomplished</u> all objectives of the new media implementation plan

AMELIORATE

{also use in Accomplishments and Achievements, Accountability, Attention to
Detail, Creativity, Leadership, Learn, Novel and Adaptive Thinking, and Self-
Manageable}

(1)   correct a mistake; improve; make better; tolerate

(2)   correct a deficiency or defect; make right a wrong; take action that makes
      up for one's negative or improper actions

Résumé bullet points:

- • <u>Ameliorated</u> years of serious customer service failures by better recruiting and hiring, quality training, and a results-based compensation plan

ASCERTAIN

{also use in Accountability}

(1)   determine; discover; establish; find out; learn; realize; uncover

(2)   find out with certainty

   *(1), (2) I <u>ascertained</u> the extent of the high levels of product failure and
   determined its cause and devised a cost effective solution.*

<u>Collocates to: attempt, degree, desire, difficulty, extent, facts, need, order,
sequence, truth</u>

Résumé bullet points:

- • <u>Ascertained</u> the long-term impact on market share of reducing advertising, which led to the decision to continue the advertising campaign

ASCRIBE

{also use in Accountability, Attention to Detail, Computational Thinking,
Honesty, and Integrity}

(1)   accredit; arrogate; assert that something has been caused by someone or
      something; attribute something to someone

   *(1) The increase in global sales is <u>ascribed</u> to the general economic
   recovery.*

Collocates to: attributes, belief, characteristics, feeling, meaning, phenomenon, qualities, traits, value, view

Résumé bullet points:

- Ascribed a purely political motive to FDC sanctioning of firm's mining practices

ASSIGN

{also use in Accountability, Computational Thinking, and HARD SKILLS: Administrative and Operational}

(1) allocate; allot; choose; consign; dispense; dole out; give; hand over; pick; select; transfer

(2) appoint; delegate; designate; detail; name
Résumé bullet points:

- Assigned the responsibility to meet and greet dignitaries and escort them to company events

- Assigned cross-discipline individuals to project management teams

AUTHENTICATE

{also use in Accountability}

(1) confirm; endorse; serve to prove; substantiate; validate
Résumé bullet points:

- Authenticated $50 million of customer claims of financial loss due to firm's investment advice

DEFINE

{also use in Accomplishments and Achievements, Accountability, Attention to Detail, Critical Thinking and Problem Solving, Design Mind-Set}

(1) characterize; classify; describe; determine or set boundaries; distinguish; identify; label; term

(2) circumscribe; delimitate; delimit; demarcate; mark out
Résumé bullet points:

- Defined the parameters of the firm's adoption of a value chain strategy

EARMARK

{also use in Accountability, Attention to Detail, Commitment and Dedication, and Time Management}

(1) allocate; allot; appropriate; assign; reserve for special purpose; set aside

(2)   mark the ears of livestock for special identification

Collocates to: assets, funds, money, process, projects, reforms, requests, spending

Résumé bullet points:

  • <u>Earmarked</u> donations for appropriate causes, ensuring continued flow of
    funds

EFFECTUATE

{also use in Commitment and Dedication and Learn}

(1)   bring about; cause or accomplish something; effect

   *(1) The positive change in company morale was <u>effectuated</u> by strong
   investor interest.*

Collocates to: change, goals, intent, necessity, plans, policy, purpose, resources, standards

ELUCIDATE

{also use in Accountability}

(1)   clarify; explain; explicate; expose; expound; illuminate; lucid; make
       something clear; reveal; throw light on

   *(1) I was able to <u>elucidate</u> the results and findings of the complex
   research study and make them clear to the Board of Directors.*

Collocates to: help, needs, research

ENSURE

{also use in Accountability}

(1)   follow; guarantee; make certain; make sure

(2)   make safe; protect; secure

Résumé bullet points

  • <u>Ensured</u> that all staff were given proper training in social media
    techniques

  • <u>Ensured</u> accurate, timely delivery of customer orders

  • <u>Ensured</u> that firm maintained competitive edge in marketplace by con-
    ducting continual customer satisfaction research

IMPUTE

{also use in Accountability}

(1) accredit; ascribe a result or quality to anything or anyone; assign; attribute; fix

(2) accuse; allege; assert; challenge; charge; cite; implicate

(2) The accreditation committee <u>imputed</u> the school's graduation rates.

<u>Collocates to: costs, date, datasets, income, policy, regulations, value</u>

SANCTION

{also use in Accountability}

(1) abet; authorize; confirm; countenance; give official permission; permit; ratify

(2) impose penalty

(2) The firm's in-house counsel was <u>sanctioned</u> by the American Bar Association.

ATTENDANCE AND PUNCTUALITY

Attendance and punctuality is the ability to consistently be where one has committed to be or is supposed to be and be on time.

ACCOUNT FOR

{also use in Analytical, Attention to Detail, HARD SKILLS: Business Sense, and Research Computational}

(1) analyze; at hand; available; consider; explain to know the state of or whereabouts of something or someone

Résumé bullet points:

• <u>Accounted for</u> 25 percent of new hires

ASSEMBLE

(1) accumulate; combine; convene; group; mass produce; produce standardized goods in large volumes; unite

Résumé bullet points:

• <u>Assembled</u> project team in one week, a team that achieved two breakthrough projects in 2012

ATTEND

(1)   be counted; be there; show up
Résumé bullet points:

- Attended all meetings of the Board of Directors as the employee liaison

SCHEDULE

(1)   make arrangements or a plan for carrying out something

(2)   plan events and activities for certain times
Résumé bullet points:

- Scheduled all the president's visits with global stakeholders

- Scheduled fulfillment of all mail orders and managed customer return issues

ATTITUDE, APPROACHABILITY, AND PERSONALITY

Attitude is an individual's apparent view and evaluation of something. It can be favorable or unfavorable of something or someone and determines how comfortable others are in interacting with the individual.

ABREACH

{also use in Communications}

(1)   release repressed emotions by acting out in words or behavior based one's imagination of the situation

(1) The negotiations had reached such a hostile tone that everyone was surprised and relieved when the firm's chief negotiator abreached decorum and stood on the conference table and sang.

ACHIEVE

{also use in Accomplishments and Achievements, Drive and Passion, Education, Leadership, Motivated, Novel and Adaptive Thinking, Risk Tolerant, Self-Confidence}

(1)   accomplish; attain; complete; conclude; do; finish; get; perform; pull off; reach; realize

(2)   succeed in doing something
Résumé bullet points:

- Achieved the firm's first industry productivity award in 2011

ACQUIESCE

{also use in Accountability, Cognitive Load Management, Compassion, and Social Intelligence}

(1)   accept; agree; assent; comply with passively; concede; concur; consent; give in; go along with; submit; yield

   (1) It was an important sign of personal growth for Joe to <u>acquiesce</u> to a plan to which he originally did not agree.

Collocates to: agree, accept, compelled, expect, forced, should, would

Résumé bullet points:

   • <u>Acquiesced</u> to new owners to save more jobs

ADAPT TO CHANGE

(1)   acclimate; accommodate; adjust; change; conform; fashion; fit; get used to; make suitable; reconcile; square; suit; tailor

   (1) The ability to <u>adapt to change</u> is an important characteristic that employers look for in applicants.

(2)   make fit, often by modification

(3)   cause something to change for the better

Résumé bullet points:

   • <u>Adapted to change</u> in a highly volatile business environment with grace and professionalism

AVER

(1)   affirm; assert the truthfulness of something; avow; claim; declare; maintain; profess; state; swear

Résumé bullet points:

   • <u>Averred</u> all technological claims in firm's marketing and promotional materials

CHOPE

(1)   reserve something such a seat, place, or book

   (1) It's free seating at the concert, so we need to get there early to <u>chope</u> seats for our group.

COMPORT

(1)   act; agree; behave in a certain way that is proper

   (1) My staff was always the group that <u>comported</u> to department dress codes.

CORUSCATE

(1)   brilliant in style; flashy; showy; sparkle

(1) The graphics of the advertisement <u>coruscated</u> through my mind.

COUNSEL

{also use in Communication, Compassionate, and Social Intelligence}

(1)   advise; deliberate; inform
Résumé bullet points:

• <u>Counseled</u> new hires on company guidelines regarding branding issues

DISABUSE

(1)   correct; enlighten; free one from an incorrect assumption or belief

(1) My white paper <u>disabused</u> the critic's assertion that our products were unsafe.

EXHORT

(1)   admonish strongly; encourage earnestly by advice or warning; insist; press; push; urge

(1) "I <u>exhort</u> you also to take part in the great combat, which is the combat of life, and greater than every other earthly combat."

—Plato

MELIORATE

(1)   improve; make something better
Résumé bullet points:

• <u>Meliorated</u> the interdepartmental disagreements between sales and customer service, thus reducing a major factor in employee turnover and low morale

MOLLIFY

(1)   appease; calm; pacify; placate; soften; soothe

(1) My comments on the new policy <u>mollified</u> the employees who saw it as a negative.

Résumé bullet points:

• <u>Mollified</u> the most vitriolic of consumers who had waited in line for days for the product

PERSEVERE

(1) be steadfast in purpose; continue in some effort or course of action in spite of difficulty or opposition; persist

(1) "Victory belongs to the most <u>persevering</u>."

—Napoleon

Résumé bullet points:

- <u>Preserved</u> the firm's ten-year record of double-digit sales growth by completing the IBM sale three months ahead of forecast

PROPITIATE

(prō pis/h´ē āt´)

(1) favor; gain approval; like best; placate; win over

(1) We <u>propitiated</u> stakeholders by keeping them informed about key decisions.

<u>Collocates to: decision makers, directors, leaders, managers, people, stakeholders</u>

RATIOCINATE

(ras/h´ē äs ənāt´)

{also use in Design Mind-Set, and HARD SKILLS: Accounting and Finance}

(1) sagacious; work toward a solution through logical thinking and reason

(1) My <u>ratiocinated</u> approach helped a previously divided staff to accept the new policy as beneficial to the health of the firm and to their job security.

RECRUDESCE

(1) become active again after a period of latency; break out

(1) This ingenious marketing plan <u>recrudesced</u> this slumbering organization.

SEAGULL

(1) hang back and await an opportunity to benefit from desirable circumstances found or created by other people

(1) Some would say he was wily or even devious, but David <u>seagulled</u> and always benefited from the success of others.

TEMPER

(1)   make more temperate, acceptable, or suitable; restrain

(2)   bring to a desired consistency, texture, or hardness by a process of grad-
ual heating and cooling

*(1), (2) "We dare not forget today that we are the heirs of that first revo-
lution. Let the word go forth from this time and place, to friend and foe
alike, that the torch has been passed to a new generation of Americans—
born in this century, <u>tempered</u> by war, disciplined by a hard and bitter
peace, proud of our ancient heritage, and unwilling to witness or permit
the slow undoing of those human rights to which this nation has always
been committed, and to which we are committed today at home and
around the world."*

—John F. Kennedy, Presidential Inaugural Address, Washington, D.C.,
January 19, 1961

VENERATE

(1)   honor as scared or noble; respect deeply; revere

(2)   look upon with feelings of deep respect; regard as venerable

(1), (2) He was and is greatly <u>venerated</u> in the health care field.

APPEARANCE AND PERSONAL HYGIENE

One's personal appearance and hygiene is the state, condition, or manner in
which one appears; it is a person's outward look.

ACCESSORIZE

(1)   add ornaments to; beautify; decorate; do up; furnish with accessories;
refurbish; renovate

(2)   wear or select accessories

*(1), (2) The way she <u>accessorized</u> herself indicated she had vast knowl-
edge of fashion.*

ADORN

(1)   bedeck; bedizen; deck out; decorate; dress up; embellish; garnish;
ornament; trim

*(1) The graduate students were <u>adorned</u> with the new blazers and
scarves.*

BEDAZZLE

(1)   adorn; beautify; dress up

(1) We were <u>bedazzled</u> by the appearance, technology, and presentation of the sponsor.

BEDECK

(1)   decorate something or someone

(1) The salesmen were <u>bedecked</u> with company blazers, fedoras, and leather briefcases.

CLEAN UP WELL

(1)   dress and look much better than normal; surprise others with one's put-together appearance

(1) Tom looked dashing in his tux; he <u>cleaned up well</u> for the board reception, having come off an oil rig just three hours ago.

INCANDESCE

(1)   beam; emit a light; flame; glow; shine

(1) The student choir <u>incandesced</u> in their beautiful robes with the special back lighting.

LIFE STREAM

(1)   record or broadcast one's continuous or streaming daily activities by means of a digital device that is part of one's glasses or clothing

(1) In the future, archeologists won't have to interpret cave paintings because they will have our history, which we <u>life streamed</u> by digital audio and graphic recordings of daily activities from the mundane to really significant human activities of our time.

MASK

(1)   disguise something; hide real meaning of something

(1) John <u>masked</u> his lack of self-confidence by playing the clown figure.

OGLE

(1)   eyeball; gaze at; look at; look at in an amorous or impertinent way; observe; stare at; watch

(1) The audience <u>ogled</u> the panel of models.

OVERDRESS

(1)   be conspicuous at an event or activity because one is dressed in clothing too formal for the occasion

(1) A job applicant showing up for an interview <u>overdressed</u> can be a problem.

PREEN

(1)   make one's self look attractive; tidy and clean

(1) He <u>preened</u> before every presentation because he knew the importance of the visual package.

SUIT UP

(1)   dress in the proper uniform or outfit for an event or contest

(1) He <u>suited up</u> in preparation for the event.

TITIVATE

(1)   adorn; dress up; put finishing touch on; spruce up

(1) If she had not <u>titivated</u>, she would not have felt as confident for the presentation.

ATTENTION TO DETAIL AND ACCURACY

ABOUND

(1)   flourish; present in large numbers; teem with; thrive

(2)   be fully supplied; be plentiful; be rich and abundant; have plenty of; proliferate

Collocated to: concerns, ideas, opportunities, problems, questions, signs, theories, thoughts

ABSORB

{also use in Accomplishments and Achievements, Accountability, Cognitive Load Management, Common Sense, Commitment and Detail, Cross-Cultural Competency, Flexibility, Learn, and Self Manageable}

(1)   acquire; assimilate; attract; consume; digest; endure; engulf; fascinate; imbibe; soak up; sustain; take in; use up

(2)   draw into oneself; grasp; realize; recognize; take in; understand

(3)   become captivated, interested, engaged, or preoccupied in; fascinated
Résumé bullet points:

- <u>Absorbed</u> two underperforming units into my department and still met all yearly objectives

ABSTERGE

(1)   clean; cleanse; purge; wipe away

ACCENTUATE

{also use in Accountability, Accuracy, and Preciseness, Cognitive Load Management, Commitment and Dedication, Communication, Creativity, Drive and Passion, Leadership, and Motivated}

(1)   accent; emphasize; heighten; intensify

(2)   make more noticeable; play up; stress something
Résumé bullet points:

- <u>Accentuated</u> the firm's civic accomplishments in all PR activities

ACCLIMATE

(1)   acclimatize; accustom yourself; adapt; adjust; become accustomed to a new environment or situation; familiarize; get used to
Résumé bullet points:

- <u>Acclimated</u> to the new corporate culture following the merger and won accolades from new management

ACCOMPLISH

{also use in Accomplishments and Achievements, Accountability, Accuracy and Precision, Drive, Passion and Tenacity, Leadership, Motivated, Novel and Adaptive Thinking, and Work Ethic}

(1)   achieve; attain; bring about; carry out; cause to happen; complete; do; gain; get done; finish; fulfill; make happen; make possible; produce; pull off; reach; realize; undertake
Résumé bullet points:

- <u>Accomplished</u> the most difficult parts of the industry certification while managing two departments
- <u>Accomplished</u> all assignments on time and within budget guidelines

ACCOUNT FOR

{also use in Attendance and Punctuality, Analytical, Computational, and HARD SKILLS: Business Sense and Research}

(1)   be responsible for; get the credit or blame for

(2)   analyze; at hand; available; consider; explain

(3)   know the state of or whereabouts of something or someone
Résumé bullet points:

> • Accounted for 20 percent of new sales for the division in 2012

> • Accounted for all employees in the aftermath of the 2006 earthquake

ACCREDIT

{also use in Accountability, Customer Awareness, Reliability, and HARD SKILLS: Administration and Organizational}

(1)   approve; attribute; authorize; give credit to; endorse; recognize; sanction

> *(1)   The program was accredited by the appropriate professional bodies.*

(2)   certify; supply with credentials or authority
Collocates to: colleges; courses, education, fully; ideas, institutions, programs, schools

ACT ON

(1)   accomplish; acquit yourself; be active; behave; do something; operate; proceed; react; respond; take action; take steps; work

(2)   act out; appear in; feign; impersonate; mock; perform; play in; pretend; simulate
Résumé bullet points:

> • Acted on all customer complaints within 24 hours

ACTUALIZE

{also use in Accomplishments and Achievements, Common Sense, Motivated, and Novel and Adaptive Thinking}

(1)   make real or actual; realize

(2)   fulfill the potential of
Résumé bullet points:

> • Actualized virtual transactions, giving customers a human contact

ACTUATE

{also use in Accomplishments, Achievements, Creativity, Customer Awareness, Leadership, and Risk Tolerant}

(1)   activate; arouse to action; motivate; put into motion; start; trigger
Résumé bullet points:

- Actuated the industry's first global fraud alert system, helping firms reduce their losses due to fraud by millions of dollars a year

ADAPT

{also use in Accomplishments and Achievements, Commitment and Dedication, Common Sense, Creativity, Cross-Cultural Competency, Flexibility, Learn, and HARD SKILLS: Engineering, R&D}

(1)   acclimate; accommodate; adjust; change; conform; fashion; fit; get used to; make suitable; reconcile; square; suit; tailor

(2)   make fit, often by modification

(3)   cause something to change for the better
Résumé bullet points:

- Adapted the CAD technology to firm and improved assembly line productivity by 33 percent

ADDRESS

{also use in Communications and Self-Manageable}

(1)   direct one's attention to; discourse; lecture; remark; speak directly to; talk to

(2)   deliver; direct; dispatch; forward; mark with a destination; refer

(3)   adopt; attend to; concentrate on; deal with; focus on; take up
Résumé bullet points:

- Addressed every employee complaint within two days

AFFIRM

{also use in Accountability, Critical Thinking and Problem Solving, and Honesty and Integrity}

(1)   acknowledge; affirm; announce; assert; asseverate; avow; confirm; establish; insist; pronounce; state; validate; verify

(2)   encourage; support; sustain; uphold

Résumé bullet points:

> • Affirmed the firm's First Amendment rights of commercial free speech in congressional hearings

ALIGN

{also use in Commitment and Dedication, Design Mind-Set, Self-Manageable, and Social Intelligence}

(1) ally; adjust; bring oneself into agreement with; correct; level; parallel; straighten

(2) arrange something in reference with something else
Résumé bullet points:

> • Aligned personal goals and objectives with those of the corporation

AMELIORATE

{also use in Accomplishments and Achievements, Accountability, Accuracy and Preciseness, Creativity, Leadership, Learn, Novel and Adaptive Thinking, and Self-Manageable}

(1) correct a mistake; improve; make better; tolerate

(2) correct a deficiency or defect; make right a wrong; take action that makes up for one's negative or improper actions
Collocates to: conditions, effects, efforts, problems, situations, symptoms

ANALYZE

{also use in Critical Thinking, HARD SKILLS: Analytical, Research, Computational, and Gather Data and Convert into Information}

(1) consider; dissect; evaluate; examine; explore; interpret; investigate; probe; question; scrutinize; study
Résumé bullet points:

> • Analyzed firm's results and proposed loss prevention plan that saved $280,000 in the first year of implementation

ASCERTAIN

(1) determine; discover; establish; find out; learn; realize; uncover

(2) find out with certainty

> *(1), (2) My research ascertained the sources responsible for theft of company intellectual property worth $17 million.*

Résumé bullet points:

- Ascertained the most accurate cost of an industrial sales call, since McGraw Hill stopped publishing the data in the 1980s, thus providing a more accurate figure of the cost of sales

ASCRIBE

{also use in Accountability, Accuracy and Preciseness, Computational Thinking, Honesty and Integrity}

(1) accredit; arrogate; attribute something to someone; assert that something has been caused by someone or something

(1) Many of the health benefits ascribed to the product were proven by my research.

Collocates to: attributes, meaning, motives, powers, tendencies, traits, qualities, values

ASSEVERATE

{also use in Cognitive Load Management, Communications, and Design Mind-Set}

(1) assert; aver; avouch; avow; declare earnestly or solemnly; hold; maintain

(1) He asseverated that the mistakes in the report would be corrected.

ATTRIBUTE

(1) accredit; ascribe; assign; attach; classify; credit to; connect; designate; impute; lay at someone's door; make part of

(1) The drop in revenue was attributed to marketplace confusion regarding replacement parts.

AUDIT

{also use in Accounting and Finance, Computational Thinking, and Design Mind-Set}

(1) appraise; assess; check; count; examine; inspect; review; verify the accounting records of

Résumé bullet points:

- Audited the company's books and filed all tax forms

AUTHENTICATE

(1)   confirm; endorse; serve to prove; substantiate; validate
Résumé bullet points:

- Authenticated all digital coupons sent in by vendors valued at $45 thousand

AVER

{also use in Critical Thinking and Problem Solving and Honesty and Integrity}

(1)   affirm; assert the truthfulness of something; avow; claim; declare; maintain; profess; state; swear
Résumé bullet points:

- Averred all technological claims in firm's marketing and promotional materials

BALANCE

{also use in Accountability, Critical Thinking and Problem Solving, and Cross-Cultural Competency}

(1)   assess; calculate; collate; compare; consider; evaluate; even out; equalize; keep upright; offset; settle; square; stabilize; stay poised; steady; tally; total; weigh; weight up

(1) My management style balanced the financial needs of the firm and the human needs of the employees.

Résumé bullet points:

- Balanced personal and work goals with effective time and organizational management skills

BATTLE TEST

(1)   test something in a real-world situation; test something under the most difficult of conditions

(1) The rock crusher was battle tested in severe weather conditions.

BENCHMARK

{also use in Design Mind-Set, Learn, Professional Demeanor, and HARD SKILLS: Advertising, Branding, PR, Sales, and Marketing, and HARD SKILLS: Business and Business Sense}

(1)   commence; identify and learn from the best business practices; level point of reference; standard; target

Résumé bullet points:

- <u>Benchmarked</u> a dozen new marketing measurements that provided previously unused method to determine effectiveness
- <u>Benchmarked</u> specifications for systems implementation

BLUE PENCIL

(1)   censor; correct or edit writing, as if by changing or deleting; cross out

(1) I personally <u>blue penciled</u> the construction plans.

BOWDLERIZE

(1)   censor; edit; expurgate; remove obscenity or other inappropriate content

(1) When the CEO got involved with Web content, he didn't just edit it; he <u>bowdlerized</u> it.

CALENDERIZE

(1)   arrange by date; organize; program
Résumé bullet points:

- <u>Calenderized</u> every industry conference and seminar so employees could identify and select the events that suited their schedules, thus saving hundreds of man-hours

CALIBRATE

(1)   adjust; attune; mark gradations; measure properly; regulate; standardize
Résumé bullet points:

- <u>Calibrated</u> all the firm's purchases of used lab equipment following ISO 17025 standards

CATEGORIZE

{also use in Accountability, Creativity, and Critical Thinking}

(1)   assort; classify; separate
Résumé bullet points:

- <u>Categorized</u> all the products into their appropriate NAICs categories

CENTRALIZE

{also use in Design Mind-Set and HARD SKILLS: Administrative and Organizational}

(1)   consolidate; bring power of something to the central organization
Résumé bullet points:

   • <u>Centralized</u> the functions of 11 regional sales offices, streamlining
     reporting functions

CERTIFY

{also use in Design Mind-Set; Honesty and Integrity, and Reliability}

(1)   assure; attest; confirm; testify; verify; vouch; witness
Résumé bullet points:

   • <u>Certified</u> the inspection work of the quality control team

CHERRY-PICK

(1)   choose the best thing; choose something very carefully; elect; opt; single
      out

   *(1) Because we had first choice, we were able to <u>cherry-pick</u> the best
   interns.*

CITE

(1)   mention; name; proof; quote; refer or quote authority
Résumé bullet points:

   • <u>Cited</u> as "Top Performer" in Best 100 Systems Analysts in trade journal

CLASSIFY

{also use in Computational Thinking and Gather Data and Convert into
Information}

(1)   arrange; assort; catalog; categorize; class; distribute to groups; grade;
      group; list by some order or sequence; organize; sort
Résumé bullet points:

   • <u>Classified</u> the firm's 17,000 products into industry categories, making
     reorder, fulfillment, and shipping more efficient and less expensive

CONCATENATE

(kən kat´n āt´)

(1)   integrate; link together; unite or join in a series or chain

   *(1) The volunteers <u>concatenated</u> to form an old-fashioned bucket brigade
   to fight the fire.*

COORDINATE

{also use in Accomplishments and Achievements, Critical Thinking, HARD SKILLS: Administer and Organizational, and Problem Solving}

(1) bring together; combine; direct; harmonize; manage; match up; organize; synchronize; work together

Résumé bullet points:

- Coordinated complex, multinational research projects for global research department

- Coordinated the translation of all company PR, branding, and marketing materials from English to Spanish

CORRELATE

{also use in Computational Thinking, Cross-Cultural Competency, and HARD SKILLS: Analytical, Research, and Computational}

(1) associate; calculate or show the reciprocal relation between; come together; bring into mutual relation; correspond; parallel

(1) The survey data indicated that the two factors were strongly correlated.

CORROBORATE

(1) back; back up with evidence; confirm formally; make certain the validity of; strengthen; support a statement or argument with evidence

(1) My report corroborated the initial results of the Board Ethics Committee.

Collocates to: allegations, details, evidence, findings, information, observations, results, rumors, stories

DEDUCE

{also use in Critical Thinking and Problem Solving and Learn}

(1) assume from observations; conclude from evidence; conjecture; figure out; hypothesize; infer; presume; posit; reason; suppose; surmise; suspect; work out

(1) The consulting team deduced from its observations that the firm needed to build brand.

(2) trace the course of deviation

DEFINE

{also use in Accomplishments and Achievements, Accountability, Accuracy and Preciseness, Critical Thinking and Problem Solving, Design Mind-Set}

(1)   characterize; classify; describe; determine or set down boundaries; distinguish; identify; label; term

(2)   circumscribe; delimit; delimitate; demarcate; mark out

Résumé bullet points:

- Defined the levels of experience and skill set necessary for all job openings

DELIMIT

{also use in Critical Thinking and Problem Solving, Design Mind-Set, and Time Management}

(1)   define; demarcate; determine; fix boundaries; restrict; set limits; state clearly

(1) The research was delimited to ensure that no data was gathered on children under 13 years of age.

DELINEATE

{also use in Accountability, Attention to Detail, and Communication}

(1)   describe accurately; determine; draw an outline; identify or indicate by marking with precision; fix boundaries; represent something

Résumé bullet points:

- Delineated the limits of expense account approvals for managers

DEMARCATE

(1)   separate clearly; set boundaries; set mark

Résumé bullet points:

- Demarcated a transaction boundary to define a unit of work

DETAIL

(1)   allocate; describe; itemize; list; note; notify; particularize; specify

(1) The marketing plan detailed the approaches to be taken to reach the new marketplace.

(2)   assign; conscript; delegate; designate; order

Résumé bullet points:

- <u>Detailed</u> the funding request for the SBA-backed loan

DISABUSE

(1)   correct; enlighten; free one from an incorrect assumption or belief
<u>Collocates to: beliefs, ideas, notions, plans, thoughts, views</u>

EARMARK

{also use in Accountability, Accuracy and Preciseness, Commitment and Dedication, and Time Management}

(1)   allocate; appropriate; assign; allot; set aside; reserve for a special purpose

(2)   mark the ears of livestock for special identification

   (1), (2)   The new funds were <u>earmarked</u> for global expansion.

Résumé bullet points:

- <u>Earmarked</u> the excess of profits over budget for employee bonuses

EDIT

{also use in Accountability, Communication, and Take Directions}

(1)   alter; correct; revise and make ready

(2)   prepare a written work for publication by selection, arrangement, and annotation

(3)   make additions, deletions, or other changes
Résumé bullet points:

- <u>Edited</u> the company newsletter for eight years

EDUCATE

{also use in Communications, Intelligence, and Learn}

(1)   provide knowledge in a particular area

(2)   discipline; edify; inform; impart knowledge; instruct; mentor; teach; train; tutor

(3)   develop and train the innate capacities of by schooling or education
Résumé bullet points:

- <u>Educated</u> new vendors about the firm's view of the value chain relationship

EDUCE

{also use in Cognitive Load Management, Critical Thinking and Problem Solving, Intelligence and Leadership}

(1)   come to conclusion; derive; evoke; solve a problem based on thoughtful consideration of facts

(2)   deduce; draw out; elicit; infer

(3)   bring out or develop; elicit from

FOCUS

(1)   apply one's attention to; concentrate; intent; pay close attention to something

Résumé bullet points:

    • <u>Focused</u> on managing toward results

IDENTIFY

(1)   associate; empathize; make out; mark; recognize; relate; place; point out with certainty; see

(2)   categorize; classify; name

(3)   ascertain; designate; detect; discover; find; isolate; pinpoint

(4)   distinguish; make something stand out; set apart; single out

Résumé bullet points:

    • <u>Identified</u> new acquisition targets for the firm, thus enabling the company to become one of the state's largest businesses

INTEGRATE

(1)   articulate; concatenate; make part of; include as part of whole; unify

Résumé bullet points:

    • <u>Integrated</u> the outside and inside sales teams, reducing duplicative activities, marketplace confusion, and costs

INTERPRET

{also use in Intelligence}

(1)   construe; explain; present in understandable terms; represent the terms of individual belief or judgment; tell the meaning of

Résumé bullet points:

- Interpreted the impact of all proposed Federal regulations on the business, giving the strategic planning group advanced planning time and keeping us ahead of the competition

JUXTAPOSE

(1)   adjoin; place side by side or close together for purposes of comparison; put side by side to compare

(1) The two products were juxtaposed for the prospect to judge.

METHODIZE

(1)   order; organize; systematize
Résumé bullet points:

- Methodized asset management and inventory of equipment and software, creating annual cost savings of $400,000

NUANCE

(1)   give nuance to; provide subtle difference or degree of distinction
Résumé bullet points:

- Nuanced nonverbal and verbal cues in all speeches to maximize impact

ORCHESTRATE

{also use in Accountability and Design Mind-Set}

(1)   combine and adapt to obtain a particular outcome

(2)   arrange or organize surreptitiously to achieve a desired effect
Résumé bullet points:

- Orchestrated the change in strategic direction by emphasizing the market potential in aftermarket products, increasing the company's profits by 17 percent

PERSEVERATE

{also use in Design Mind-Set and Reliability}

(1)   continue something; repeat something insistently or over and over again

(1) The subjects in this study perseverated.

PINPOINT

(1)   find or locate exactly; identify; isolate; pin down
Résumé bullet points:

- Pinpointed gaps in marketplace penetration, allowing a more effective and efficient reallocation of resources and retargeting of marketing efforts

PRIORITIZE

(1)   sequence or sort by importance
Résumé bullet points:

- Prioritized niche market opportunities with research so resources could be more effectively allocated

PROFILE

(1)   describe something; offer details of
Résumé bullet points:

- Profiled and segmented existing customers and created prioritized prospect model that reduced the ratio of sales calls to close by 25 percent, saving hundreds of dollars per call

QUANTIFY

{also use in Critical Thinking and Problem Solving, and HARD SKILLS: Accounting and Finance, and Analytical, Research, and Computational}

(1)   express something in quantifiable terms

(2)   explanation provided as a numerical expression

(3)   determine or express or explain the quantity of, numerical measure of, or extent of
Résumé bullet points:

- Quantified transferable experience and skills of job applicants into a reliable interview application, identifying the highest potential of success

SCHEDULE

{also use in Time Management}

(1)   make arrangements or a plan for carrying out something

(2)   plan events and activities for certain times

Résumé bullet points:

- <u>Scheduled</u> all fulfillment, including orders, and managed all customer return issues

SYNTHESIZE

(1)   combine into a coherent whole; summarize the whole; provide an abstract of the whole

Résumé bullet points:

- <u>Synthesized</u> circuits to meet required specifications

TABULATE

{also use in Computational Thinking, HARD SKILLS: Accounting and Finance, and Analytical, Research, and Computational}

(1)   add up; chart; count; put facts in a table or column tally; total

Résumé bullet points:

- <u>Tabulated</u> and analyzed data from all customer focus groups

VET

(1)   check someone's suitability for security clearance; examine, evaluate

Résumé bullet points:

- <u>Vetted</u> all employees selected for top security clearances

COGNITIVE LOAD MANAGEMENT

Cognitive Load Management is the ability to filter and differentiate information for importance and to understand how to maximize cognitive functions using a variety of tools and techniques.

ABDUCE

(1)   advance evidence for; allege; cite

(1) The analysis and interpretation of the survey's data <u>abduced</u> the Theory of Business.

ABSORB

{also use in Accomplishments and Achievements, Accountability, Common Sense, Commitment and Detail, Cross-Cultural Competency, Flexibility, Learn, and Self-Manageable}

(1)   acquire; assimilate; attract; consume; digest; endure; engulf; fascinate; imbibe; soak up; sustain; take in; use up

(2)   draw into oneself; grasp; realize; recognize; take in; understand

(3)   become captivated, interested, engaged, or preoccupied in; fascinated
Résumé bullet points:

- Absorbed three unprofitable stores and still made annual sales and profit objectives

ABSTRACT

{also use in Intelligence}

(1)   detach; draw away from; extract; remove; select; separate; take out

(2)   abridge; condense; pre[as]cis; purloin; shorten; take or extract the relevant or important information from; summarize; synopsize
Collocates to: context, data, information, knowledge, manner, social

ACCENTUATE

{also use in Accountability, Accuracy and Preciseness, Attention to Detail, Commitment and Dedication, Communication, Creativity, Drive and Passion, Leadership, and Motivated}

(1)   accent; emphasize; heighten; intensify

(2)   play up; make more noticeable; stress something

(3)   mark with an accent
Collocates to: differences, figures, negatives, positives, shapes

Résumé bullet points:

- Accentuated differences in product quality

ACCLIMATE

{also use in Common Sense, Cross-Cultural Competency, Flexibility, Leadership, Learn, Novel and Adaptive Thinking, Professional Demeanor, Team Player, and Work Ethic}

(1)   acclimatize; adapt; accustom yourself; adjust; become accustomed to a new environment or situation; familiarize; get used to

ACQUIESCE

{also use in Attitude, Compassion, and Social intelligence}

(1)   accept; agree; assent; comply with passively; concur; concede; consent; give in; go along with; submit; yield

(1) The management team <u>acquiesced</u> and allowed the extra holiday to be a paid day off.

Collocates to: authority, choices, customs, demands; laws, regulations, rules

ADJUDICATE

{also use in Accountability, Critical Thinking, and Design Mind-Set}

(1)   act as judge; listen; mediate; preside over argument; settle
Résumé bullet points:

- <u>Adjudicated</u> the disputes between staff scientists over the experiment procedures

ADUMBRATE

{also use in Leadership and Risk Tolerant}

(1)   foreshadow; give a general description of something but not the details; prefigure; obscure; overshadow; predict; presage; summary

(1) She <u>adumbrated</u> the global financial problem based on her years of experience as an international financial consultant.

ALLUDE

(1)   casually and indirectly refer; covert; indicate; introduce; make an implication; suggest; talk about; touch on

(1) He <u>alluded</u> to the agreement in his speech.

ANNOTATE

(1)   comment on; critically note or comment; explain; interpret; make notes on
Résumé bullet points:

- <u>Annotated</u> the literature reviews of research interns

ASSEVERATE

{also use in Attention to Detail, Communications, and Design Mind-Set}

(1)   assert; aver; avouch; avow; declare earnestly or solemnly; hold; maintain

(1) He <u>asseverated</u> that the theory of relativity would be confirmed by actual evidence.

ASSIST

{also use in Compassionate, Self-Manageable, and Team Player}

(1)   abet; collaborate; facilitate; help with

Résumé bullet points:

- Assisted the new product development team with research activities

ASSUAGE

(əswāj´)

(1)   apease; erase doubts and fears; mollify; pacify; satisfy; soothe

(1) The last holdouts on the Board of Directors were finally assuaged to support the new plant construction by the report on market needs.

BLUE SKY

{also use in Communication and Motivation}

(1)   out of the box, strategic, long-range thinking; visionary thinking

(1) Once the committee arrived at the retreat, they went into planning groups and blue skied the possibilities of the new product concept.

BOOST

(1)   advance; amplify; augment; enhance; further; heighten; hoist; improve; increase; lift; make better; raise

Résumé bullet points:

- Boosted output of the plant by 20 percent within a year after assuming the duties of plant manager

BRAINSTORM

(1)   come up with; devise; dream up; generate ideas; think strategically

(1) Our project management team brainstormed the idea and came up with six potential uses.

Résumé bullet points:

- Brainstormed for ways to perform total quality customer service

COALESCE

{also use in Accountability, Accomplishments and Achievements, Commitment and Dedication, Cross-Cultural Competency, Flexibility, Leadership, Learn, Social Intelligence}

(1)   combine; come together as one; grow together; join; unite

*(1) The project management team <u>coalesced</u> around the sponsor's
suggestions.*

COGITATE

(1)   consider; deliberate; meditate; muse; ponder; reflect; ruminate

(1) She <u>cogitated</u> deeply before deciding to take the offer.

COLLATE

{also use in Accomplishments and Achievements, Design Mind-Set, Team
Player, and HARD SKILLS: Gather Data and Convert to Information}

(1)   assemble or collect to compare; bring together; gather; pool; pull together
Résumé bullet point:

- <u>Collated</u> data obtained from customer surveys into an improvement
  tracker

CONCEPTUALIZE

{also use in Cognitive Load Management, Communications, Leadership, and
Learn}

(1)   interpret something from the abstract; create an understandable point out
      of a concept
Résumé bullet points:

- <u>Conceptualized</u> the entire security network around Cisco protocol and
  equipment

DEDUCT

(1)   abstract; remove; subtract; take; take away; withhold

(2)   deduce; infer; posit

(2) I <u>deducted</u> the solution based on similar variables in other situations.

DEMYSTIFY

(1)   clear up; clarify; eliminate or remove mystery; make rational or compre-
      hensible
Résumé bullet points:

- <u>Demystified</u> the capabilities of nanotechnologies

DEPICT

{also use in Accountability and Communications}

(1) describe; get a picture of; give a picture of; illustrate; picture in words; portray; present a lifelike image; represent; show

DEVELOP SOFTWARE

(1) envision and write/code computer instructions to perform desired functions

Résumé bullet points:

• <u>Developed software</u> to run the firm's invoicing needs for 2,500 industrial customers

DISENTANGLE

{also use in Design Mind-Set and Self-Manageable}

(1) clear; free from entanglements and ties; find solutions to problems; straighten out

(1) Her insights and negotiating skills <u>disentangled</u> the otherwise complicated situation.

EDIFY

{also use in Communications, Compassionate, Intelligence, Learn, and Social Intelligence}

(1) educate; enlighten; illuminate; improve; inform; instruct; teach

(2) uplift morally, spiritually, or intellectually

(1), (2) The speaker's message <u>edified</u> and raised the spirits of everyone in attendance.

EDUCE

{also use in Attention to Detail and Accuracy, Critical Thinking and Problem Solving, Intelligence and Leadership}

(1) come to conclusion; solve a problem based on thoughtful consideration of facts; derive; evoke

(1) It was <u>educed</u> from the analysis of the focus groups that our advertising message was not achieving its goal.

(2) draw out; elicit; infer; deduce

(3) bring out or develop

ELUCIDATE

{also use in Accountability, Communication, Social Intelligence, HARD SKILLS: Analytical, Research, and Computational, and Take Direction}

(1)   clarify; explain; explicate; expose; expound; illuminate; lucid; make something clear; reveal; throw light on it

Résumé bullet points:

   • <u>Elucidated</u> cloud computing

EXTRAPOLATE

{also use in Cogitative Load Management and HARD SKILLS: Analytical, Research, and Computational}

(1)   construct an image; estimate; infer

(2)   arrive at conclusion or results by hypothesizing from known facts or observations

   (2) The business model was <u>extrapolated</u> from Schumpeter's work.

GARNER

(1)   accumulate; acquire; assemble; bring together; bunch up; collect; gain; gather; get; harvest; heap; earn; reap

   (1) We <u>garnered</u> a great deal of information about our competitors from the surveys.

HYPOTHESIZE

{also use in Critical Thinking and HARD SKILLS: Analytical, Research, and Computational}

(1)   educated guess of some outcome

   (1) The researchers <u>hypothesized</u> that there was a connection between consumer loyalty and employee satisfaction.

IMBIBE

{also use in Intelligence and Learn}

(1)   receive in the mind and retain; soak; steep; take in

   (1) Repetition advertising <u>imbibed</u> viewers with slogans, jingles, and themes that were supposed to come into their attention unexpectedly.

LUCUBRATE

(1)   apply one's mind to acquiring knowledge; study

   (1) He <u>lucubrated</u> by dedicating himself to nearly constant learning.

OBVIATE

(1)   anticipate to prevent difficulties or disadvantages; avert; hinder; preclude; prevent

   (1) Disaster was <u>obviated</u> because a risk management plan was in place.

Résumé bullet points:

   • <u>Obviated</u> disasters by implementing risk management

PERCEIVE

(1)   become aware or conscious of through the senses; distinguish; identify; make out; notice; pick out; regard as

(2)   observe; remark; see; take in

(3)   comprehend; feel; sense; realize

Résumé bullet points:

   • <u>Perceived</u> the need for a more accurate and qualitative gap analysis

POSIT

{also use in Accountability, Critical Thinking and Problem Solving, and HARD SKILLS: Analytical, Research, and Computational}

(1)   assume; conceive; conjecture; hypothesize; imagine; postulate; put forward; speculate; suggest; state or assume as fact; theorize

   (1) The consultants <u>posited</u> a far different short-term outlook than the board strategic committee.

SEGUE

{also use in Self-Manageable and Time Management}

(1)   continue without break; lead into new areas; proceed without interruption; smooth change to next topic

   (1) I found a less costly approach that more easily <u>segued</u> the OEM process.

COMMON SENSE, STREET SMARTS

Common sense is the ability for one to perceive the current situation, environment, or facts and then make a careful and sensible decision or judgment.

ABIDE

{also use in Accountability, Commitment and Dedication, Cross-Cultural Competency, Professional Demeanor and Presence, Reliability, Self-Manageable, and Work Ethic}

(1)   bear; continue; endure; go on being; put up with; stomach; take; tolerate

(2)   hold; remain; stand fast; stand for; stay

(3)   remain with someone; stay
Collocates to: agreements, conditions, laws, norms, rules; resolutions, wishes

ABSORB

{also use in Accomplishments and Achievements, Accountability, Attention to Detail and Accuracy, Cognitive Load Management, Commitment and Dedication, Cross-Cultural Competency, Flexibility, Learn, and Self-Manageable}

(1)   acquire; assimilate; attract; consume; digest; endure; engulf; fascinate; imbibe; sustain; soak up; take in; use up

(2)   draw into oneself; grasp; realize; recognize; understand

(3)   become captivated, interested, engaged or preoccupied in; fascinated
Résumé bullet points:

   • Absorbed 15 percent price increases from vendors and still maintained prices for customers

ACCLIMATE

{also use in Cognitive Load Management, Cross-Cultural Competency, Flexibility, Leadership, Learn, Novel and Adaptive Thinking, Professional Demeanor, Team Player, and Work Ethic}

(1)   acclimatize; accustom yourself; adapt; adjust; become accustomed to a new environment or situation; familiarize; get used to

   (1) The proper combination of reading and trial and error may be the best approach to get new people acclimated to the rigors of the job.

ACCOMMODATE

{also use in Accomplishments, Compassionate, Cross-Cultural Competency, Customer Awareness, Flexibility, and Outgoing}

(1)   house; lodge; provide accommodations; put up

(2)   adapt; be big enough for; contain; have capacity for; hold; reconcile; seat

(3)   do a favor or a service for someone

(4)   adjust; become accustomed; familiarize; get used to; make suitable

(5)   allow for; assist; be of service; consider; find ways to help; oblige

Résumé bullet points:

- Accommodated diversity input when developing business strategy

ACTUALIZE

{also use in Accomplishments and Achievements, Attention to Detail, Motivated, and Novel and Adaptive Thinking}

(1)   make real or actual; realize

(1) The business plan actualized the dream of the entrepreneurs.

(2)   fulfill the potential of

ADAPT

{also use in Accomplishments and Achievements, Attention to Detail, Commitment and Dedication, Creativity, Cross-Cultural Competency, Flexibility, Learn, and HARD SKILLS: Engineering and R&D}

(1)   acclimate; accommodate; adjust; change; conform; fashion; fit; get used to; make suitable; reconcile; square; suit; tailor

(2)   make fit, often by modification

(3)   cause something to change for the better

Résumé bullet points:

- Adapted the fleet of delivery trucks to use propane, thus saving $100,000 a year on gasoline

ADJUST

{also use in Accountability, Cross-Cultural Competency, Engineering, Flexibility, R&D, and Work Ethic}

(1)   accommodate; alter; amend; attune; bend; change; correct; fine-tune; fix; modify; pacify; regulate; resolve; rectify; settle; tune up; tweak

Résumé bullet points:

- Adjusted to new regulations

ANTICIPATE

(1)   await; be hopeful for; discussion or treatment; expect; foresee and deal with in advance; give advance thought; look forward to; think likely; wait for

Résumé bullet points:

- <u>Anticipated</u> the global slowdown of Rare Earth metals a year and built a stockpile that carried us through until production picked up

BACKSTOP

{also use in Commitment, Dedication, and Work Ethic}

(1) be a type of insurance to ensure that the security issue will be purchased

(2) act as a backstop; use as a measure of last resort in case of an emergency
Résumé bullet points

- <u>Backstopped</u> more than $500 million in stock and bond issues

BOOTSTRAP

{also use in Design Mind-Set and Self-Manageable}

(1) initiative; manage without assistance; succeed with few resources
Résumé bullet points:

- <u>Bootstrapped</u> own start-up company

BUMP THE SHARK

{also use in Drive and Passion}

(1) push back against an aggressive person; stand up against an intrusive, aggressive, or assertive verbal assault

(2) fight back against a bully

(1), (2) Sandra surprised everyone when she <u>bumped the shark</u> and put Jason in his place.

CHOP WOOD

(1) work hard; make an extra effort

(1) We <u>chopped wood</u>, never quit, and climbed the mountain, and the results showed our effort.

COWBOY UP

{slang}

(1) accept life as it happens; act like a man in the face of hardships

(2) accept punishment and defeat with stoic resolve

(1), (2) Ron <u>cowboyed up</u> after letting everyone down and showed his true colors.

CROWD SOURCE

{also use in Advertising}

(1) identify a group with common demographic or psychographic characteristics and determine how to best make contact with them to deliver a message such as a sales or advertising message

Résumé bullet points:

- Crowd sourced 300,000 prospects by Facebook and Meetup

DISCOVER

{also use in Accomplishments and Achievements, Critical Thinking and
Problem Solving, Gather Data and Convert into Information, and Intelligence}

(1) ascertain; be first to learn something; determine; expose; find out; hear;
learn; realize, see, or uncover something

Résumé bullet points:

- Discovered an untapped global demand for used car parts

FERRET OUT

(1) search and discover through persistent discovery

Résumé bullet points:

- Ferreted out the weak links in our touted value chain approach and kept
all key accounts

GIN UP

{also use in Accomplish and Self-Confidence}

(1) create; encourage; produce; increase

(1) *It is easy to get ginned up about some of the new technology.*

GREASE THE SKIDS

(1) help ease or prepare the way for someone

(1) *It was my pleasure to have greased the skids for such a deserving
young person.*

JERRY-RIG

(1)   construct a device in a crude or unstructured manner; solve a problem with creative use of only materials at hand

(1) The maintenance team jerry-rigged a loading platform to keep the operation going in the emergency.

JOCKEY

(1)   arrange to get into a better position; maneuver; position for something
Collocates to: advantage, for place, position, power, space, with

JUMP-START

(1)   bring to life; get a project moving by bypassing normal procedures; get going; kick-start; pop the clutch
Résumé bullet points:

  • Jump-started Internet start-up by crowd funding

KICK THE TIRES

(1)   first to investigate; look for or check for early warning signs; look into something by checking the obvious things
Résumé bullet points:

  • Kicked the tires of global merger deals

PULL THE TRIGGER

(1)   go ahead after thinking and planning; make the final decision to act or do something; no going back

(1) She pulled the trigger on the controversial plan and showed why she is considered one of the top CEOs in the field.

TACKLE

(1)   encounter; engage; face; take hold of; take on

(2)   deal with a difficult person or situation
Résumé bullet points:

  • Tackled problems as they arose, not letting situations get worse than when they appeared

COMMITMENT AND DEDICATION

Commitment and Dedication involve someone's personal pledge to make an obligation of his time, energy, or resources to do something and continue until the task or obligation is fulfilled.

ABET

{also use in Accountability, Learn, Motivated, and Social Intelligence}

(1) advocate; assist; back; back up; encourage; espouse; foment; help incite; put up to; sanction; support; urge (especially in wrongdoing)

(1) We <u>abetted</u> in the decision to go ahead with the controversial design.

ABIDE

{also use in Accountability, Common Sense, Cross-Cultural Competency, Motivated, Professional Demeanor and Presence, Reliability, Self-Manageable, and Work Ethic}

(1) bear; continue; endure; go on being; put up with; stomach; take; tolerate

(2) hold; remain; stand fast; stand for; stay

(3) remain with someone

Collocates to: agreements, conditions, laws, norms, rules; resolutions, wishes

ABSORB

{also use in Accountability, Attention to Detail and Accuracy, Cognitive Load Management, Common Sense, Cross-Cultural Competency, Learn, and Self-Manageable}

(1) acquire; assimilate; attract; consume; digest; endure; engulf; fascinate; imbibe; sustain; soak up; take in; use up

(2) draw into oneself; grasp; realize; recognize; understand

(3) become captivated, interested, engaged, or preoccupied in; fascinate

Résumé bullet points:

• <u>Absorbed</u> underperforming departments and still achieved budget goals

ACCEDE

{also use in Accountability, Customer Awareness, Flexibility, Outgoing, and Social Intelligence}

(1) agree; allow; approach; ascend; attain; come to; comply; conform; consent; enter upon; give assent; grant; succeed to; take over

Résumé bullet points:

- Acceded to requests of stakeholders

ACCELERATE

{also use in Accomplishments and Achievements, Motivated, Self-Manageable, Time Management, and HARD SKILLS: Time and Organizational Management}

(1)   gather speed; go faster; grow; hurry; increase speed of; pick up the pace; quicken; rush; speed up;

(2)   cause to occur sooner

Résumé bullet points:

- Accelerated time-to-market for new products by 20 percent through use of "Breakthrough Project Management" methodology

ACCENTUATE

{also use in Accountability, Accuracy and Preciseness, Attention to Detail, Cognitive Load Management, Leadership, Communication, Creativity, Drive and Passion, Leadership, and Motivated}

(1)   accent; emphasize; heighten; intensify

(2)   make more noticeable; play up; stress something

    (1), (2) The decision was <u>accentuated</u> with a round of applause.

(3)   mark with an accent

ACTIVATE

{also use in Accomplishments and Achievements, Critical Thinking and Problem Solving, and Novel and Adaptive Thinking}

(1)   acetify; become active; energize; galvanize; get going; initiate; make active; start; set in motion; set off; stimulate; trigger; turn off

Résumé bullet points:

- Activated stovepipe plans

ADAPT

{also use in Accomplishments and Achievements, Attention to Detail, Common Sense, Creativity, Cross-Cultural Competency, Flexibility, Learn, and HARD SKILLS: Engineering and R&D}

(1)   acclimate; accommodate; adjust; change; conform; fashion; fit; get used to; make suitable; reconcile; square; suit; tailor

(2)   make fit, often by modification

(3)   cause something to change for the better

Résumé bullet points:

- <u>Adapted</u> the in-house training program to include more emphasis on employees' civic responsibilities

ADOPT

{also use in Accomplishments and Achievements, and Accountability}

(1)   accept; agree to; assume; approve; choose; embrace; endorse; espouse; foster; implement; take in as one's own; take on; take on board; take up

Résumé bullet points:

- <u>Adopted</u> only those new technologies that made organization more effective

ADVOCATE

{also use in Compassion, Self-Manageable, and Reliability}

(1)   advance; back; be in favor of; bolster; defend; encourage; promote; sponsor; support

Résumé bullet points:

- <u>Advocated</u> for truth in advertising long before it became a catch phrase

ALIGN

{also use in Attention to Detail, Design Mind-Set, Self-Manageable, and Social Intelligence}

(1)   ally; adjust; bring oneself into agreement with; correct; level; parallel; straighten

(2)   arrange something in reference with something else

Résumé bullet points:

- <u>Aligned</u> and trained two sales groups, creating more customer contact points

ASSUAGE

(1)   appease; erase doubts and fears; mollify; pacify; satisfy; soothe

(1) I <u>assuaged</u> the concerns of the staff by sharing with them all the information I had.

BACKSTOP

{also use in Common Sense and Work Ethic}

(1)   act as a backstop; provide last-resort support or security in a securities offering for the unsubscribed portion of shares; use as a measure of last resort in case of an emergency

Résumé bullet points:

- Backstopped 100 percent of $30 million of unsubscribed shares

BRING ABOUT

{also use in Design Mind-Set}

(1)   be the reason for; cause

Résumé bullet points:

- Brought about a passion for quality in every position

CAMPAIGN

(1)   battle; canvass; crusade; engage; fight; hold an operation; participate; push; struggle

Résumé bullet points:

- Campaigned for more customer focus in all operations in every job

CARRY THE WATER

{also use in Customer Awareness, Leadership, Self-Confidence, and Work Ethic}

(1)   bear the main responsibility for something; manage something for others by oneself

Résumé bullet points:

- Carried the water for new product idea

CHAMPION

{also use in Accountability, Leadership, Novel and Adaptive Thinking, and Self-Confidence}

(1)   advocate; back; campaign for; crusade for; excel; fight for; stand up for; support; uphold; be a winner

Résumé bullet points:

- Championed development of software simulation and modeling methods to assist marketing in determining that customer's "voice" procedure is now SOP

COALESCE

{also use in Achievements, Accomplishments, Accountability, Cognitive Load Management, Cross-Cultural Competency, Flexibility, Leadership, Learn, Social Intelligence, and Team Player}

(1)   come together as one; combine; grow together; join; unite
Résumé bullet points:

  • Coalesced previous group of individuals into something more than the sum of the parts

COLLABORATE

{also use in Accomplishments and Achievements, Communication, Cross-Cultural Competency, Self-Manageable, Take Direction, and Work Ethic}

(1)   act as a team; assist; cooperate; pool resources; team up; work jointly with; work together
Résumé bullet points:

  • Collaborated with hundreds of vendors and suppliers to ensure value chain proposal met all customer needs

COMMIT

(1)   confide; consign; dedicate; devote to a special task or purpose; entrust; perpetuate; pull off; relegate
(2)   fill a future obligation
(3)   put an insane or mentally incapable person in charge of another
Résumé bullet points:

  • Committed 100 percent effort to every endeavor

COMPLETE

{also use in Accomplishments and Achievements, Accountability, Education, Self-Manageable, and Work Ethic}

(1)   be done; choate; conclude; entire; finish a task intact; integral; perfect; through; unabridged; uncut; whole; wrap up
Résumé bullet points:

  • Completed twice the organization's requirement for civic projects annually for five consecutive years
  • Completed successful branding repositioning by developing new branding platform, logo, and message points that accurately capture and identity organization's personality, values, and objectives

COMPORT

(1)   act; agree; behave in a certain way that is proper
Collocates to: brilliantly, herself, himself, themselves, with
Résumé bullet points:

- Comported with professionalism in all business dealings

COOPERATE

{also use in Social Intelligence}

(1)   act together; agree; associate; co-adjudge; collaborate; social capital;
work together for a common purpose
Résumé bullet points:

- Cooperated with internal auditors to identify cost savings

CULTIVATE

{also use in Customer Awareness, Intelligence, Self-Manageable, and Social
Intelligence}

(1)   develop; encourage; foster; help; nurture; promote; refine; support

(2)   tend to; till; work on
Résumé bullet points:

- Cultivated winning attitude on teams managed

CUSTOMIZE

{also use in Creativity and Engineering, Research and Development}

(1)   build or fit according to individualized specifications
Résumé bullet points:

- Customized in-house training modules

DEDICATE

(1)   apply; bestow; devote; donate; give; grant; offer; set apart

(2)   commit; consecrate; surrender
Résumé bullet points:

- Dedicated all efforts to the organization's mission

DEVOTE

{also use in Compassionate}

(1)   allocate; allot; apply; bestow; confer; consecrate; dedicate; hallow; lavish
Résumé bullet points:

   • <u>Devoted</u> all personal efforts to accomplishing the organization's mission

EARMARK

{also use in Accountability, Accuracy and Preciseness, Attention to Detail, and
Time Management}

(1)   allocate; appropriate; assign; allot; set aside; set aside or reserve for special purpose

(2)   mark the ears of livestock for special identification

(3)   set a distinctive mark on
Résumé bullet points:

   • <u>Earmarked</u> the funds for shareholder dividends

EFFECTUATE

{also use in Accuracy and Preciseness and Learn}

(1)   bring about; cause or accomplish something; effect

   *(1) The new Board of Directors <u>effectuated</u> the rebuilding plan that had
   been on the table for years.*

<u>Collocates to: change, goals, intent, necessity, plans, policy, purpose,
resources, standards</u>

ELUCBRATE

{also use in Communications}

(1)   produce a written work through lengthy, intensive effort

   *(1) Years of research and thousands of interviews <u>elucbrated</u> the
   classic work.*

EMEND

(1)   correct or edit; remove faults in a scholarly or literary work; improve

   (1) Ronnie <u>emended</u> the year-end report.

HUNKER DOWN

{also use in Work Ethic}

(1) become determined not to budge from an opinion or position; circle the wagons; get in defensive position; prepare for bad news or prolonged assault; prepare for siege; protect your boss from outsiders

(1) The campaign committee hunkered down to plan its next strategy.

PERSEVERE

{also use in Reliability}

(1) be steadfast in purpose; continue in some effort or course of action in spite of difficulty or opposition; persist

(1) New businesses start-ups that persevered during the recession should have long-term survivability.

COMMUNICATION, SPEAKING, WRITING, LISTENING, AND NONVERBAL CUES

Communication is the exchange of ideas, thoughts, feelings, information, data, knowledge, and messages by speech, writing, visual depictions, or behavior.

ABREACT

{also use in Personal Hygiene and Appearance and Accountability}

(1) release repressed emotions by acting out in words, behavior, or imagination

(1) He abreacted with an emotional dialogue.

ACCENTUATE

{also use in Accountability, Accuracy and Preciseness, Attention to Detail, Cognitive Load Management, Leadership, Commitment and Dedication, Creativity, Drive and Passion, Leadership, and Motivated}

(1) accent; emphasize; heighten; intensify

(2) make more noticeable; play up; stress something

(3) mark with an accent

Résumé bullet points:

  • Accentuated the differences between products and the competition

ADDRESS

{also use in Attention to Detail and Self-Manageable}

(1) direct one's attention to; discourse; lecture; speak directly to; remark; talk to

(2) deliver; direct; dispatch; forward; mark with a destination; refer

(3) adopt; attend to; concentrate on; deal with; focus on; take up

Résumé bullet points:

- Addressed long-standing and deep-rooted ineffective system procedures

ADDUCE

(1) allege; bring forward; cite as evidence; lead to; present; put forward

Résumé bullet points:

- Adduced evidence that networking was the most effective job searching tool

ADJURE

{also use in Take Direction}

(1) beg; change under oath; renounce under oath; request earnestly

ADVERTISE

(1) amplify; brand; broadcast; communicate; disseminate; inform; market; notify; present; promote; publicize; recommend; sell

(2) send paid communications through media channels to audiences that are most likely interested in the product, service, idea, or concept to which the advertising is referring

Résumé bullet points:

- Advertised for new employees through peer networks and frequently found excellent candidates

ALLUDE

(1) covert; casually and indirectly refer; indicate; introduce; make an implication; suggest; talk about; touch on

(1) The CEO alluded to the changes in his speech.

ANSWER

{also use in Social Intelligence}

(1)   come back with; counter; react; reply; respond; rejoin; retort

(2)   explain one's actions or behavior

(3)   fulfill; lay to rest; meet; resolve; satisfy; solve
      Résumé bullet points:

> • Answered own phone in three rings or less and answered all emails
>   within 24 hours

ARTICULATE

{also use in Processional Demeanor}

(1)   be eloquent; express; be fluent; communicate; convey; be lucid; put into
      words; state; tell; verbalize
Résumé bullet points:

> • Articulated a detailed technology roadmap for wireless Java

ASSEVERATE

{also use in Attention to Detail, Cognitive Load Management, and Design
Mind-Set}

(1)   assert; aver; avouch; avow; declare earnestly or solemnly; hold; maintain

> *(1) She asseverated eloquently.*

ATTEST

{also used in Honesty and Integrity}

(1)   certify, witness, or swear to

> *(1) The product claims were attested to by three independent sources.*

AUTHOR

{also use in Accomplishments and Achievements and Creativity}

(1)   create; pen; scribe; source; write
Résumé bullet points:

> • Authored six books
> • Authored paper for publication

BANDY ABOUT

(1)   discuss casually usually among friends

> *(1) The political issues were bandied about during the break-in session.*

BANTER

(1)   challenge; joke; mock; poke fun at; ridicule; talk without purpose; tease

(1)   The sales team <u>bantered</u> with the accounting team about the viability of some accounts.

BLANDISH

(1)   cajole; coax; influence; induce or persuade by gentle flattery

(1)   Felix <u>blandished</u> Diana with complaints about her recent business success.

BLAZON

(1)   advertise; proclaim something widely

(1)   The new product must be <u>blazoned</u> to get the consumer attention it needs.

BLOG

(1)   publically accessible personal journal in digital format

(2)   weblog

Résumé bullet points:

   • <u>Blogged</u> about industry issues

BRAINSTORM

(1)   come up with; dream up; devise; generate ideas freely; think; think strategically

Résumé bullet points:

   • <u>Brainstormed</u> solutions with cross-departmental teams

CAJOLE

{also use in Motivated}

(1)   blandish; coax; entice; flatter; inveigle; soft-soap; sweet-talk; wheedle

(1)   Not all employees respond to positive motivation; some need to be <u>cajoled</u>.

CHRONICLE

(1)   account; diary; history; narrative; journal; record; register; story

Résumé bullet points:

   • <u>Chronicled</u> the industry's fight against the piracy of intellectual property

COMMUNICATE

(1)   be in touch; connect; converse; correspond; convey something; exchange a few words; share; write

Résumé bullet points:

- <u>Communicated</u> proactively with team members via media to share information, coordinate meeting notes, and help team members with individual assignments
- <u>Communicated</u> with ease and confidence

COMPOSE

(1)   collect; contain; control; cool down; practice; restrain; settle; simmer down

(2)   create; incite; produce; write

Résumé bullet points:

- <u>Composed</u> freelance articles

CONCEPTUALIZE

{also use in Communications, Leadership, and Learn}

(1)   create an understandable point out of a concept; interpret something from the abstract

(1) The copywriters <u>conceptualized</u> the benefits from the product prototypes.

CONSTRUE

(1)   analyze something in a certain way; explain; infer or deduce; interpret; translate

(1) It is easy to see how someone could have <u>construed</u> that conclusion from the limited information that was released.

CONSULT

(1)   ask; check with; confer; consider; discuss; see; seek advice from; sound out; talk things over

(2)   check in; look up; refer to; turn to

Résumé bullet points:

- <u>Consulted</u> and recommended operational improvements

CONVEY

{also use in Analytical, Research, and Computational}

(1)   conduct; express; lead; make known; pass; put into words

    (1) Roberto <u>conveyed</u> the board's offer to the candidate.

(2)   bring; carry; move; take from one place to another; transfer

CONVOKE

(1)   assemble; call together; convene; summon to a meeting

    (1) David <u>convoked</u> a member's business meeting at the annual conference to challenge the board action.

COUNSEL

{also use in Attitude, Compassionate, and Social Intelligence}

(1)   advise; deliberate; inform

Résumé bullet points:

    • <u>Counseled</u> young people on the dangers of misusing social media

DEBATE

(1)   argue a point strongly; put forth reasons for or against contest; deliberate; discuss; question

(2)   consider; contemplate; deliberate; mediate; ponder; think over; weigh in; wonder

Résumé bullet points:

    • <u>Debated</u> the globalization issue with those seeking to close US markets

DELINEATE

{also use in Accountability, Attention to Detail, and HARD SKILLS: Analytical, Research, Computational}

(1)   describe accurately; determine; draw an outline; identify or indicate by marking with precision; fix boundaries; represent something

Résumé bullet points:

    • <u>Delineated</u> the responsibilities and roles of volunteers.

DENOTE

(1)   announce; designate; indicate; mean; represent; signify; symbolize

    (1) This cooperation <u>denotes</u> a third-party affiliation agreement

(2)   allude to; convey; express; imply; refer to

DEPICT

{also use in Accountability and Cognitive Load Management}

(1)   describe; get a picture of; give a picture of; illustrate; picture in words; portray; present a lifelike image; represent; show

    (1) The brochure <u>depicted</u> the product in several applications.

DIALOGUE

(1)   chat; discourse; discuss; hold a conversation; talk

    (1) Customers <u>dialogued</u> with marketing representatives by way of a web conference.

DISABUSE

(1)   correct; enlighten; free one from an incorrect assumption or belief

    (1) As Director of Public Relations, I <u>disabused</u> writers and editors of misunderstandings and misconceptions they had of our business.

DULCIFY

(1)   ease someone's anger; make pleasant or agreeable; mollify; pacify; sweeten

    (1) After the meeting, I <u>dulcified</u> several staff who thought the CEO's remarks were attacks on them.

EARWIG

(1)   attempt to influence or insinuate oneself through flattery

    (1) Of course, I used every tactic at my disposal; I cajoled, I <u>earwigged</u>, I even pleaded—anything to make the case.

(2)   pester with private persuasion and warnings

EDIFY

{also use in Cognitive Load Management, Compassionate, Intelligence, Learn, and Social Intelligence}

(1)   educate; enlighten; illuminate; improve; inform; instruct; teach

(2)   uplift morally, spiritually, or intellectually

   (1), (2) The book edified everyone who read it.

EDIT

{also use in Accountability, Attention to Detail, Communications, and Take Directions}

(1)   alter; correct; revise and make ready

(2)   prepare a written work for publication by selection, arrangement, and annotation

(3)   make additions, deletions, or other changes
Résumé bullet points:

   • Edited the company's monthly newsletter

EDUCATE

{also use in Attention to Detail, Intelligence, and Learn}

(1)   discipline; edify; inform; impart knowledge; instruct; mentor; teach; train; tutor

(2)   develop and train the innate capacities of by schooling or education

(3)   provide knowledge in a particular area
Résumé bullet points:

   • Educated 178 vendors regarding what was expected of them in the value chain arrangement

ELABORATE

(1)   amplify; develop; enlarge; expand on

   (1) The field manual elaborated on the procedures covered in the packing instructions.

(2)   complex; complicate; convolute; dilate; expatiate on; fancy; intricate; provide detail on

(3)   produce by effort

(4)   develop in great detail; work out carefully

ELICIT

(1)   bring out; call forth something; extract; obtain

(2)   cause to be revealed; draw forth; evoke

(1), (2) The new product elicited a variety of positive and negative responses.

ELUCBRATE

{also use in Commitment and Dedication}

(1)   produce a written work through lengthy, intensive effort

(1) Twenty researchers and five writers elucbrated for five years to produce the guide book.

ELUCIDATE

{also use in Accountability, Communication, HARD SKILLS: Analytical, Research, and Computational, Social Intelligence, and Take Direction}

(1)   clarify; explain; make something clear; explicate; expose; expound; illuminate; lucid; reveal; throw light on something of interest

(1) The consultant elucidated on the benefits of employing professional guidance.

EMBELLISH

(1)   adorn; aggrandize; elaborate

(2)   adorn with gimcrack or gimmick or gimmickry; decorate or improve by adding detail or ornamentation

(3)   improve an account or report of an event by adding factious, imaginary, or audacious details to improve or heighten the acceptance of; touch up

(1), (2), (3) The products were embellished with a lot of things that did not really add much value.

ENUMERATE

(1)   catalog; count off; itemize; list; tally

(2)   determine the number of; total

(3)   name one by one; specify

(1), (2), (3) The packing list enumerated each of the 300 parts.

EVINCE

(1)   reveal or indicate the presence of a particular feeling or condition; show plainly

(2)   indicate; make manifest without a doubt

(1), (2)   The staff <u>evinced</u> during the open staff meetings.

EXPATIATE

{also use in Reliability}

(1)   cover a wide scope of topics; elaborate

(2)   add details to an account or an idea

(3)   roam or wander freely

(4)   speak or write in great detail

(1-4)   Our CEO <u>expatiated</u> at the annual meeting and ran over his time by 1 hour.

EXPOUND

(1)   expand; explain or interpret; develop; put forward for consideration; set forth point by point; state in detail

(1) The union rep <u>expounded</u> the benefits of a union shop in a full employee meeting.

EXTOLL

(1)   admire; exalt; glorify; laud; magnify; praise

(1) Jackie's boss <u>extolled</u> her work during the annual performance review.

FACEBOOK

{also use in New Media Literacy and HARD SKILLS: Computer Literacy}

(1)   connect with someone online on the social network Facebook

(1) Many of our vendors, suppliers, and customers are <u>Facebooked</u>.

FACILITATE DISCUSSION

(1)   direct, lead, monitor, or guide a group discussion
Résumé bullet points:

• <u>Facilitated discussion</u> with management about the advantages of telecommuting

GLEAN

(1)   collect; extract; gather something bit by bit

   (1) Jorge <u>gleaned</u> a great deal of customer data from the census.

ILLUSTRATE

(1)   adorn; clarify; enlighten; explain; make understandable; represent

   (1) Our annual report <u>illustrated</u> in graphics our mission and vision.

IMPART

(1)   bestow a quality; communicate; convey; disclose; divulge; expose; give a share or portion; inform; instruct; make known; pass on; report; reveal; teach; tell

   (1) The CEO <u>imparted</u> the firm's vision in his annual message.

IMPLY

(1)   connote; entail; infer; hint; indicate; involve necessarily; point to; mean; purport; signify; suggest without stating directly

   (1) Some advertising we used <u>implied</u> certain benefits.

INFORM

(1)   direct; guide

(2)   bring up to date; enlighten; let authorities know; notify; report; tattle; update

   (1), (2) The best software packages keep users <u>informed</u> about updates and changes.

INNERVE

{also use in Self-Confidence and Social Intelligence}

(1)   call to action; provoke; stimulate something

   (1) The FDC rules <u>innerved</u> the industry and provoked an emergency meeting of leaders.

INTERJECT

(1)   butt in; cut in; exclaim; interpose; interrupt; introduce; put or set into between another or other things; speak; throw in

   (1) Tom <u>interjected</u> additional thoughts that were not in his prepared notes.

INTERVIEW

(1)   ask; in query; review question

(1) Sales representatives who have <u>interviewed</u> prospects rather than sell them have experienced much greater success.

JUXTAPOSE

(1)   two things adjoining and used for comparing; place side by side or close together for purposes of comparison; put side by side to compare

(1) The presenter <u>juxtaposed</u> the buyers resistance and the sellers need to close.

LAUD

{also use in Accountability, Outgoing, and Team Player}

(1)   acclaim; applaud; celebrate; extol; mention; praise; speak well of

(1) Good communicators are <u>lauded</u> for their simple but effective styles.

LISTEN

(1)   attend; hark; hear; hearken; lend an ear; list; make an effort to hear and understand something; pay attention; respond to advice, request, or command

(1) The people who are considered the best communicators are those who <u>listen</u> before they speak.

NOTE

(1)   document; jot down; log; make a note of; note down; pay attention; record in writing; record; write down

(2)   be aware of; notice; observe; take in; take note of

(1), (2) It is <u>noted</u> when you are considerate and thoughtful.

OBJECTIFY

(1)   externalize; make objective or concrete; represent an abstraction as if in bodily form

(1) Too many people have <u>objectified</u> digital content.

OPINE

(1)   discourse; go on; harangue; hold, express, or give an opinion; lecture; orate; preach; rant; stress something; speak out; suppose; think

    (1) Sandra <u>opined</u> to the other staff about the compensation plan.

OPPUNGE

(1)   challenge the accuracy, probity of

    (1) The external auditors <u>oppunged</u> our accounting records.

PARLAY

(1)   exploit an asset successfully; take a winning position and stake all on a subsequent effort

(2)   talk or negotiate with someone

    (1), (2) Our negotiators <u>parlayed</u> the news into a stronger position.

PARSE

(1)   component parts of a sentence; give out in parts or sections

    (1) He <u>parsed</u> the document, so the original meaning was altered.

PIQUE

(1)   generate curiosity or interest

    (1) Once he had <u>piqued</u> my curiosity, there was no turning back.

(2)   feeling of annoyance generated as a result of a perceived insult or injustice

(3)   excite or arouse; irritate

PONTIFICATE

(1)   blowhard; brag; express opinions in a pompous and dogmatic way

    (1) Don had <u>pontificated</u> on this topic before, so we knew beforehand what to expect.

POSTULATE

{also use in HARD SKILLS: Analytical, Research, and Computational}

(1)   assume; claim; guess; hypothesize; look for a reason or take for granted without proof; propose; put forward; suggest

Résumé bullet points:

• <u>Postulated</u> traditional price theories in cycles

PRESENT

(1) give formally or ceremonially

(2) formally introduce someone to someone else

(3) put (a show or exhibition) before the public

(4) appear formally before others

Résumé points:

• <u>Presented</u> new sales training for companywide sales force of 500 people

PROMULGATE

(1) broadcast; circulate; publish or make known; spread; transmit

(1) The company <u>promulgated</u> a written code of ethical conduct.

PROOF

(1) make a copy; read for clarity, style, and errors

(1) Harris <u>proofed</u> the copy of the ads that were going to be placed in the magazine.

PUBLISH

(1) print; post online; cause to be published

Résumé bullet points:

• <u>Published</u> online newsletter

RUMINATE

{also use in Critical Thinking and Problem Solving}

(1) chew over; cogitate; contemplate; mull over; ponder; reflect on; think over

(2) mediate; turn over in one's mind

(1), (2) When alumni got together, they <u>ruminated</u> over bygone days.

SCRUTINIZE

{also use in Critical Thinking and Problem Solving}

(1) analyze; dissect; examine carefully; inspect; pore over; search; study

(1) All content on the company Web site was <u>scrutinized</u> for proper protocol.

STYLEFLEX

{also use in Computer Literacy}

(1) attempt to adjust one's communications style to accommodate others; deliberate

(1) Too many people have <u>styleflexed</u> their communications styles.

WRITE

(1) compose something
Résumé bullet points:

* <u>Wrote</u> six books

COMPASSIONATE, CARING, KIND, EMPATHETIC

Compassion is the virtue of feeling empathy for the suffering of others.

ACCOMMODATE

{also use in Accomplishments and Achievements, Common Sense, Cross-Cultural Competency, Customer Awareness, Flexibility, and Outgoing}

(1) house; lodge; provide accommodations; put up

(2) adapt; be big enough for; contain; have capacity for; hold; reconcile; seat

(3) do a favor or a service for someone

(4) adjust; become accustomed; familiarize; get used to; make suitable

(5) allow for; assist; be of service; consider; find ways to help; oblige

Résumé bullet points:

* <u>Accommodated</u> foreign language investors

ACQUIESCE

{also use in Accountability, Attitude, Cognitive Load Management, and Social Intelligence}

(1) accept; agree; assent; consent; comply with passively; concur; concede; give in; go along with; submit; yield

(1) The committee members <u>acquiesced</u> to the chairman's point of order.

ADVISE

(1) counsel; direct; give advice; give opinion; recommend; warn

(2) inform; let know; make aware; notify; tell someone what has happened

Résumé bullet points:

> • <u>Advised</u> individual investors of their options

ADVOCATE

{also use in Communication, Self-Manageable, and Reliability}

(1)   advance; back; be in favor of; bolster; defend; encourage; promote; sponsor; support

Résumé bullet points:

> • <u>Advocated</u> for work sharing

ALLAY

{also use in Cross-Cultural Competency}

(1)   alleviate; calm; dispel; put to rest; relieve; subside

> *(1) The customer's concerns were <u>allayed</u> once the replacement piece arrived.*

ALLEVIATE

(1)   lessen; make bearable; relieve

Résumé bullet points:

> • <u>Alleviated</u> investor concerns with record earning three consecutive years

ASSENT

{also use in Team Player}

(1)   accede; accept; acquiesce; agree; concur; consent

> *(1) It would have been a different outcome if the vendor had not <u>assented</u> to the terms.*

ASSIST

{also use in Cognitive Load Management, Self-Manageable, and Team Player}

(1)   abet; collaborate; facilitate; help with

Résumé bullet points:

> • <u>Assisted</u> coworkers with social media usage

BEFRIEND

(1)   behave as a friend to someone

Résumé bullet points:

> • <u>Befriended</u> coworkers transferred from other locations

CLOSE RANKS

(1)   stand together; unite; work together

  (1) Every member of the board <u>closed ranks</u> behind the embattled CEO.

COACH

(1)   direct; drill; instruct; prepare; teach; train; tutor
Résumé bullet points:

  • <u>Coached</u> young workers on field repairs, saving time and money.

COHERE

{also use in Social Intelligence and Team Player}

(1)   bond; go together; hold fast; join together

  (1) The employees <u>cohered</u> when the news of the merger broke.

COUNSEL

{also use in Attitude, Communications, and Social Intelligence}

(1)   advise; deliberate; inform
Résumé bullet points:

  • <u>Counseled</u> terminated employees on outplacement benefits

COUNTENANCE

(1)   approve; encourage; favorably dispose; sanction; support

  *(1) In the past, fiefdoms and empire building by managers would have
  never been <u>countenanced</u>.*

DEVOTE

{also use in Commitment and Dedication}

(1)   allocate; allot; apply; bestow; confer; consecrate; dedicate; hallow; lavish
Résumé bullet points:

  • <u>Devoted</u> off-work hours to civic projects

EDIFY

{also use in Cognitive Load Management, Communications, Intelligence,
Learn, and Social Intelligence}

(1)   educate; enlighten; illuminate; improve; inform; instruct; teach

(2)   uplift morally, spiritually, or intellectually

(1), (2) The moral counseling sessions <u>edified</u> the workers.

ELEVATE

(1)   advance; improve; exalt; lift up; raise

(2)   raise the pitch, tone, or volume

(3)   raise a person in title, rank, or position

(4)   raise to a higher intellectual, moral, or spiritual position

(5)   elate; exhilarate; raise the spirits of

Résumé bullet points:

   • <u>Elevated</u> direct reports to greater responsibility whenever possible

GAVE

(1)   allot; apply; bestow; deliver; distribute; donate; gift; grant; hand off; mete out; offer; present; set aside; transfer; turn over

Résumé bullet points:

   • <u>Gave</u> regularly to corporate sponsored charities

HELP

{also use in Accomplishments and Achievements and Polite}

(1)   abet; aid; assist; benefit; change for the better; improve; succor

Résumé bullet points:

   • <u>Helped</u> establish child care center in company to assist working mothers

MENTOR

(1)   give assistance in career or business matters; provide advice or guidance

Résumé bullet points:

   • <u>Mentored</u> new and existing sales reps on customer relationship management, solutions selling, and listening skills

NURTURE

{also use in Outgoing}

(1)   cherish; provide extra care and attention in hopes of developing someone or something into full potential

Résumé bullet points:

   • <u>Nurtured</u> relationships with 200 stakeholders

SERVE

{also use in Team Player}

(1)   aid; assist; be of use; do services for; help; perform duties; treat in a certain way

    (1) The employees volunteered and <u>served</u> as tutors to students.

TUTOR

(1)   coach; educate; guide; instruct; lecture; mentor; teach; train
Résumé bullet points:

   • <u>Tutored</u> MBA students

UNIFY

{also use in Cross-Cultural Competency and Intelligence}

(1)   blend; bring together; federate; merge; solidify; tie; unite

    (1) The threat of being acquired <u>unified</u> the workers.

CREATIVITY

Creativity is the ability of someone to think in ways that are not bound by rules or previous thoughts. It can result in innovative or different approaches to a particular task or problem.

ACCENTUATE

{also use in Accountability, Accuracy and Preciseness, Attention to Detail, Cognitive Load Management, Commitment and Dedication, Communication, Drive and Passion, Leadership, and Motivated}

(1)   accent; emphasize; heighten; intensify
(2)   make more noticeable; play up; stress something
(3)   mark with an accent
Résumé bullet points:

   • <u>Accentuated</u> the visionary character of the firm with advanced Web graphics

ACTUATE

{also use in Achievements, Accomplishments, Attention to Detail and Accuracy, Customer Awareness, Leadership, and Risk Tolerant}

(1)   activate; arouse to action; motivate; put into motion; start; trigger

Résumé bullet points:

- <u>Actuated</u> the reserve contingency of $2 million to keep a plant open during the recession of 2009

ADAPT

{also use in Accomplishments and Achievements, Attention to Detail, Commitment and Dedication, Common Sense, Cross-Cultural Competency, Flexibility, Learn, HARD SKILLS: Engineering and R&D}

(1) acclimate; accommodate; adjust; change; conform; fashion; fit; get used to; make suitable; reconcile; square; suit; tailor

(2) make fit, often by modification

(3) cause something to change for the better

Résumé bullet points:

- <u>Adapted</u> a multichannel marketing approach and doubled sales in less than a year

AMELIORATE

{also use in Accomplishments and Achievements, Accountability, Accuracy and Preciseness, Attention to Detail, Leadership, Learn, Novel and Adaptive Thinking, and Self-Manageable}

(1) correct a mistake; improve; make better; tolerate

(2) correct a deficiency or defect; make right a wrong; take action that makes up for one's negative or improper actions

(1), (2) The audit <u>ameliorated</u> the department's cash flow problem.

ANIMATE

(1) give life to; give sprit and support to; quicken

(1) The new CEO was more <u>animated</u>, and the staff found it easier to communicate with her.

ARRANGE

{also use in Accountability and HARD SKILLS: Administrative and Organizational}

(1) array; authorize; catalogue; classify; fix; order; organize; position; set up

(2) make plans for something to be done

Résumé bullet points:

- <u>Arranged</u> to have all the top field salespeople meet once a year

ARRAY

{also use in Attention to Detail, Design Mind-Set}

(1)   gamut; place in an orderly arrangement; set out for display or use

(2)   marshal troops; parade; place an order

(2) The products in the booth were <u>arrayed</u> in a way that visitors could easily trial them.

(3)   dress in fine or showy attire

AUTHOR

{also use in Accomplishments and Achievements and Communications}

(1)   create; pen; scribe; source; write
Résumé bullet points:

• <u>Authored</u> the firm's first guidelines on social media

BACKCAST

(1)   describe something or sometime in the past without having seen or experienced it; reconstruct past events on the basis of the study of events or other evidence

(1) Our game designers <u>backcasted</u> certain events to provide some realism to the game.

CARVE OUT

(1)   cut; choose; divide; slice
Résumé bullet points:

• <u>Carved out</u> niche markets for special products

CATEGORIZE

{also use in Accountability, Attention to Detail and Accuracy, and Critical Thinking}

(1)   assort; catalog; classify; list; separate
Résumé bullet points:

• <u>Categorized</u> and prioritized investment options for the board finance committee

CIRCUMVENT

{also use in Risk Tolerant}

(1)   avoid; dodge; elude; evade; frustrate by surrounding or going around; get around; go around; outwit; skirt; take another route; thwart

(1) We circumvented the obstacles of international shipping by producing in local countries.

CREATE

{also use in Accomplishments and Achievements}

(1)   bring about; build; cause to come into being; compose; design; give rise to; produce

Résumé bullet points:

- Created the firm's first social media resource strategy, increasing the brand's presence worldwide

CUSTOMIZE

{also use in Committed and Dedication and Engineering, Research, and Development}

(1)   design, build, or fit according to individualized specifications

Résumé bullet points:

- Customized unique landing pages for repeat visitors to the Web site

DEPICT

{also use in Accountability, Cognitive Load Management, and Communications}

(1)   describe; get a picture of; give a picture of; illustrate; represent; picture in words; portray; present a lifelike image; represent; show

(1) We depicted our products in their actual use.

DESCANT

(1)   talk freely without inhabitation

(1) Our customers descanted in our regular open panels.

DESIGN

{also use in Accomplishments and Achievements, Creativity, and HARD SKILLS: Computer Literate, Engineering, R&D}

(1) aim; contrive; devise; intend; make designs; mean; plan; propose; set apart for some purpose

(2) conceive; construct; create; draw up blueprints or plans; fabricate; invent; originate

(3) blueprint; cast; chart; contrive; draw up; frame; intent; map; project; set out

Résumé bullet points:

- <u>Designed</u> the company logo

- <u>Designed</u> and implemented fundraising goals and strategies in conjunction with the board's leadership

DEVISE

{also use in Accomplishments and Achievements and HARD SKILLS: Engineering and Research and Development}

(1) conceive; concoct; contrive; create; design; develop; formulate; imagine or guess; invent; plan; plot; sot up; think up; work out or create something

Résumé bullet points:

- <u>Devised</u> a company-wide car pool plan that reduced the number of cars in the parking lot by 25 percent, thus reducing emissions and saving fuel costs for many workers

ENCODE

{also use in New Media Literacy}

(1) transform an idea into a set of symbols during communications process

Résumé bullet points:

- <u>Encoded</u> customer data in special-purpose binary format

ENKINDLE

(1) arouse into action; burn; excite; get something going; ignite; incite; set aflame

Résumé bullet points:

- <u>Enkindled</u> passion to succeed

ENVISAGE

(1) create a mental picture; envision; foresee; form an image in the mind; imagine; visualize

(2) confront; face

Résumé bullet points:

- Envisaged that if you can see it, you can do it

EPITOMIZE

(1) abbreviate; abridge; represent; review; serve as the image of; synopsize

(2) be the symbolic representation of; make or be an epitome of
Résumé bullet points:

- Epitomized the work ethic

INFUSE

{also use in Accountability)

(1) imbue; inculcate; ingrain; inspire; instill; introduce

(2) teach a body of knowledge or perspective

(3) fill; permeate; pervade; suffuse

(4) brew; immerse; saturate; soak; souse; steep
Résumé bullet points:

- Infused with unwavering belief in internal locus of control

INNOVATE

{also use in Engineering, R&D}

(1) begin with something new; create; derive; devise; coin; commence; instigate; invent; make; modernize; originate; remodel; renew; renovate; revolutionize; transform; update
Résumé bullet point:

- Innovated Led On-Line (ILO) format for training 3,000 global employees, improving the quality for the training experience lowering training costs by 15 percent

INSPIRE

{also use in Social intelligence}

(1) affect; arouse; encourage; excite; impel; incite; prompt; provoke; motivate; stimulate; stir
Résumé bullet points:

- Inspired by my dreams

INTERLARD

(1)   intersperse; diversify; mix together

*(1) Interlarded with new product development plans are loose concepts
and other partially conceived ideas that someday may become new
products.*

PIONEER

{also use in Accomplishments and Achievements, Drive and Passion and
Tenacity, Motivated, Self-Confidence, and Self-Manageable}

(1)   first to develop new ideas or concepts; lead the way
Résumé bullet points:

  • Pioneered the use of 3-D printing

PROTOTYPE

{also use in HARD SKILLS: Business and Business Sense}

(1)   create models and replicas of what is to be produced; think of or design a
      new product
Résumé bullet points:

  • Prototyped products for customers

REVIVIFY

(ri viv´ ə fī´)

(1)   to put new attitude, life, or vigor into a cause; revive
Résumé bullet points:

  • Revivified the truth in advertising concept by creating and overseeing the
    industries' campaign to back up all advertising claims, which led to sig-
    nificant increases in consumer confidence

SOLVE

{also use in Accomplishments and Achievements, Design Mind-Set, and
Accounting and Finance}

(1)   find a solution; settle

(2)   provide or find a suitable answer to a problem
Résumé bullet points:

  • Solved many problems that limited firm's growth in productivity with
    creative, out-of-the-box solutions

VISUALIZE

(1)   create mental impression or image of something; dream of; envisage; image; picture; see in one's mind's eye; think about

Résumé bullet points:

> • <u>Visualized</u> the solutions to many issues and problems before devising solutions

CRITICAL THINKING AND PROBLEM SOLVING

Critical thinking is thinking that questions assumptions, beliefs, and views in a way that can lead to solutions to problems.

ACCRUE

{also use in Self-Manageable}

(1)   accumulate; amass; ensue; build up; increase; mount up

(2)   come to one as a gain; amass

(3)   accrete; add; to grow by addition

Résumé bullet points:

> • <u>Accrued</u> significant credibility with consumer protection groups by being unwaveringly transparent

ACTIVATE

{also use in Accomplishments and Achievements, Commitment and Dedication, Novel and Adaptive Thinking, and HARD SKILLS: Time and Organizational Management}

(1)   acetify; become active; energize; galvanize; get going; initiate; make active; set in motion; set off; start; stimulate; trigger; turn off

Résumé bullet points:

> • <u>Activated</u> targeted cost reduction contingency during economic emergencies

ADHERE

{also use in Design Mind-Set}

(1)   affix; bond; hold; hold fast; glutamate; remain; stay; stick to something

Résumé bullet points:

> • <u>Adhered</u> to highest levels of integrity and ethics in all business dealings

ADJUDICATE

{also use in Accountability, Cognitive Load Management, and Design Mind-Set}

(1)   act as judge; adjudged; deem; listen; mediate; preside over argument; regard; rule; settle

Résumé bullet points:

- Adjudicated disputes and disagreements among members of the trade association

AFFIRM

{also use in Accountability, Attention to Detail and Accuracy, and Critical Thinking and Problem Solving}

(1)   acknowledge; affirm; announce; assert; asseverate; avow; confirm; establish; insist; pronounce; state; validate; verify

(2)   encourage; sustain; support; uphold

Résumé bullet points:

- Affirmed the firm's principles in all public relations activities

ANALYZE

{also use in HARD SKILLS: Analytical, Research, and Computational, and Gather Data and Convert into Information}

(1)   consider; dissect; evaluate; examine; explore; interpret; investigate; probe; question; scrutinize; study

Résumé bullet points:

- Analyzed and interpreted data from company surveys

ARBITRATE

{also use in Flexibility}

(1)   adjudicate; decide; intercede; judge; mediate; negotiate; pass judgment; referee; settle; sort out

Résumé bullet points:

- Arbitrated disputes between in-house and field sales representatives over key accounts

ARGUE

(1)   bicker; confront; contend; debate; disagree; dispute; fall out; fight; quarrel; row; squabble

Résumé bullet points:

- <u>Argued</u> in favor of a stronger, formal, enforceable ethics policy

ASCERTAIN

(1)   determine; discover; establish; find out; learn; realize; uncover

(2)   find out with certainty

Résumé bullet points:

- <u>Ascertained</u> the root causes of customer service failures and reduced order cancellation rates by 75 percent

BALANCE

{also use in Accountability, Attention to Detail, and Cross-Culture Competency}

(1)   assess; collate; calculate; compare; consider; equalize; evaluate; even out; keep upright; offset; settle; square; stabilize; stay poised; steady; tally; total; weigh; weight up

Résumé bullet points:

- <u>Balanced</u> the need for consumer privacy and the firm's right to collect personal identifiable information, ensuring continued revenue growth with proper consumer protection

CALIBRATE

(1)   adjust; attune; mark gradations; measure properly; regulate; standardize

(1)   The device was <u>calibrated</u> to indicate average speed.

CAPITALIZE

(1)   benefit; finance; profit from; supply funds for profit; take advantage of

Résumé bullet points:

- <u>Capitalized</u> on extensive personal network to find best candidates for newly created jobs, reducing lost opportunity costs

CATEGORIZE

{also use in Accountability, Attention to Detail and Accuracy, and Creativity}

(1)   assort; catalog; classify; list; separate

Résumé bullet points:

- <u>Categorized</u> all customers into groupings by profit contribution

COGITATE

(1)   consider; deliberate; meditate; muse; ponder; reflect; ruminate

(1) The researchers <u>cogitated</u> deeply over the questioner design.

COMPUTE

{also use in HARD SKILLS, Accounting and Finance, Computational Thinking, and Software Developing}

(1)   calculate; determine a number; equations; figure
Résumé bullet points:

- <u>Computed</u> the accurate costs of an industrial sales call when there were no industry benchmarks or standards, thus helping ensure more accurate budgeting

CONCEIVE

{also use in Accomplishments and Achievements, Accountability, and Self-Manageable}

(1)   create; envisage; imagine; invent original idea; picture; visualize

(1)   elaborate; begin life; dream; form; make up
Résumé bullet points:

- <u>Conceived</u> of solutions to problems no one believed could solved

CONSOLIDATE

{also use in Cross-Cultural Competency}

(1)   bring together; merge; strengthen; unite
Résumé bullet points:

- <u>Consolidated</u> the inside and field sales force into one department, improving productivity and reducing annual costs by $200,000

CONSTRUCT

(1)   assemble; build; contrive; create; devise; draw to specifications; erect; form; make; put up; raise

(2)   blueprint; compose; create; form; piece together; structure
Résumé bullet points:

- <u>Constructed</u> measurement matrix for business plan components, making results of each section of business plans quantifiable

CONTEMPORIZE

(1)   bring up to date; modernize; make contemporary
Résumé bullet points:

- Contemporized the look of mill outlet stores, improving overall consumer appeal, increasing consumer traffic and sales

COORDINATE

{also use in Accomplishments and Achievements, Attention to Detail, Self-
Manageable, and HARD SKILLS: Administrative and Organizational}

(1)   bring together; combine; direct; harmonize; manage; match up; organize;
      synchronize; work together
Résumé bullet points:

- Coordinated the responsibilities and work of 200 volunteers across the
  nation

CORROBORATE

(1)   back; back up with evidence; confirm formally; make certain the validity
      of; strengthen; support a statement or argument with evidence
Résumé bullet points:

- Corroborated antidotal evidence of a shift in consumer preferences with
  empirical research, giving firm ten months over the competition to
  retool and begin producing

CULL

(1)   amass; collect; gather

(2)   choose; glean; pick out; select
Résumé bullet points:

- Culled social media sites for evidence of consumer opinions on firm's
  brand

DEDUCE

{also use in Attention to Detail and Learn}

(1)   assume; conclude from evidence; conjecture; figure out; infer; presume;
      suspect; hypothesize; posit; reason; suppose; surmise; work out

   *(1) It was deduced that the greater the time a salesman spent listening
   was related to an increased possibility of getting a sale.*

(2)   trace the course of deviation

DEFINE

{also use in Accomplishments and Achievements, Accountability, Accuracy and Preciseness, Attention to Detail, and Design Mind-Set}

(1) characterize; classify; describe; determine or set down boundaries; distinguish; identify; label; term

(2) circumscribe; delimitate; delimit; demarcate; mark out

Résumé bullet points:

- Defined key market segments using psychographic segmentation techniques

DELIBERATE

{also use in Time Management, and HARD SKILLS: Administrative and Organizational}

(1) confer; consider; consult; debate; meditate; mull over; ponder; plan; reflect; think carefully; weigh carefully

Résumé bullet points:

- Deliberated and resolved project management team disputes to achieve consensus

DELIMIT

{also use in Attention to Detail, Design Mind-Set, and Time Management}

(1) define; demarcate; determine; fix boundaries; restrict; set limits; state clearly

Résumé bullet points:

- Delimited the boundaries of independent sales reps so as not to interfere with established relationships of field salespeople and their key accounts, creating greater customer satisfaction

DETERMINE

(1) agree to; bound; decide; delimit; delimitate; demarcate; discover; establish; limit; judge; mark out; measure; resolve; settle on

(2) ascertain; clarify; establish; find out; uncover

(3) affect; control; govern; influence; mold

Résumé bullet points:

- Determined the optimum balance of volume for product containers and cost per unit of production

DIAGNOSE

(1)   analyze the cause or nature of something; detect; establish; identify a
       condition; make a diagnosis; spot

Résumé bullet points:

   • <u>Diagnosed</u> recalled products and discovered the defect and devised
     repair process, which eliminated need to replace product and saved $30
     million

DISCOVER

{also use in Accomplishments and Achievements, Common Sense,
Intelligence, and Gather Data and Convert into Information}

(1)   ascertain; be first to learn something; determine; expose; find out; hear;
       learn; realize, see, or uncover something

Résumé bullet points:

   • <u>Discovered</u> the defective process that threatened a total recall and saved
     $30 million in costs

DISSUADE

(1)   advise against; deter; discourage; divert; put off; talk out of

       *(1) We were <u>dissuaded</u> from further exploration by the results of the ore
       tests.*

EDUCE

{also use in Attention to Detail and Accuracy, Cogitative Load Management,
Intelligence and Leadership}

(1)   come to conclusion; solve a problem based on thoughtful consideration of
       facts; derive; evoke

(2)   draw out; deduce; elicit; infer

(3)   bring out or develop; elicit from

       *(1-3) I <u>educed</u> from the audit that our financial position was fairly
       strong.*

ENGINEER

{also use in Time Management and HARD SKILLS: Engineering}

(1)   cause; coax; make happen

(2)   plan, construct, and manage as an engineer

(3)   guide; plan and direct skillfully; superintend

Résumé bullet points:

- Engineered, troubleshot, and documented IIS solutions; tested and administered Windows 8 Developer's pilot on 190 workstations and 5 servers

ESTABLISH CORRELATION

(1)   measure the extent to which two variables are related

Résumé bullet points:

- Established correlation between cloud-based data storage and reduced hacker attacks

ESTIMATE

(1)   appraise; approximate; assay; calculate; gauge; guess; judge; rate; reckon; respect; size up; value

(2)   form an opinion or judgment about: to judge carefully

(3)   make estimates

Résumé bullet points:

- Estimated annual energy usage

EXAMINE

(1)   analyze; assess; case; consider; explore; inspect; peruse; scrutinize; study; survey; traverse; view

(2)   investigate; inquire into; look at or into critically or methodically to find out the facts, condition, or situation

(3)   test by careful questioning or scientific inquiry

Résumé bullet points:

- Examined samples of parts provided by 200 vendor suppliers for quality assurance

EXPLICATE

(eks´pli kāt´)

(1)   analyze logically; explain; make clear; write about something at great length

(1) The primary research methodology is problem-solving itself, which often, in practice, cannot be fully explicated.

EXPLORE

(1)   delve; dig; discover; examine carefully; inquiry; investigate; look into closely; probe; scout; search

(2)   travel in an area completely new to learn about the geography, history, culture, and people

(3)   search carefully, systematically, or scientifically
Résumé bullet points:

  • Explored uses for new technology

EXPOSIT

(eks-posit)

(1)   add details to an account or idea

  (1)   The reports addendum exposited many details.

EXTRAPOLATE

{also use in Critical Thinking, and HARD SKILLS: Analytical, Research, and Computational}

(1)   construct an image; estimate; infer

(2)   arrive at conclusion or results by hypothesizing from known facts or observations
Résumé bullet points:

  • Extrapolated research data and results from other industries

FATHOM

(1)   come to understand; comprehend

  (1)   The marketing community has fathomed but a tiny part of human decision making.

FERRET OUT

(1)   search and discover through persistent discovery
Résumé bullet points:

  • Ferreted out the incorrect charges, inaccurate fees, and unsubstantiated billing by phone service provider, saving firm $4,000 monthly

FIX

{also use in Accomplishments and Achievements}

(1)   affix; arrange; assign; attach; blame; fasten; impute; pin on; place saddle; produce deep impression; secure

(2)   mend; replace; restore

Résumé bullet points:

- Fixed equipment at construction sites, saving thousands of dollars in downtime

FOLLOW THROUGH

{also use in Reliability}

(1)   continue an action or activity; finish something you have started

Résumé bullet points:

- Followed through on all initiatives

FORMULATE

(1)   articulate; contrive; create; develop; devise; draft; elaborate; express; frame; invent; make; originate; plan; prepare; put into words or expressions; verbalize; voice

Résumé bullet points:

- Formulated the blend of fuel and additives that allowed equipment to function for long periods in subzero environments

GALVANIZE

{also use in Leadership and Social Intelligence}

(1)   activate; propel someone or something into sudden action; stimulate

Résumé bullet points:

- Galvanized employees into volunteer teams during emergencies

GAUGE

(1)   determine; estimate; guess; judge something or someone; measure; standard scale or measure; weigh

Résumé bullet points:

- Gauged the changes in consumer purchasing behavior in advance of industry research

HYPOTHESIZE

{also use in Cogitative Load Management and HARD SKILLS: Analytical, Research, and Computational}

(1)   educated guess of some outcome

(1) Ever since Plato, scientists have <u>hypothesized</u> about how the brain processes information.

IMAGINE

(1)   conceive; envisage; envision; fancy; fantasize; feature; guess; image; picture; plan; scheme; see; suppose; think; vision; visualize

(1) Answers generally come to those who have <u>imagined</u> solutions to problems and opportunities.

INDUCE

(1)   bring about some action; cause; effect; encourage; make; move by persuasion or influence; tempt

(2)   bring on; generate; produce; provoke; stimulate

(1), (2) Crystals are subject to aging and mechanically <u>induced</u> noise.

INITIATE

{also use in Accomplishments and Achievements and Self-Manageable}

(1)   begin; commence; create; inaugurate; induct; install; instate; instigate; introduce; invest; kick off; open; set off; start

(2)   coach; instruct; mentor; teach; train; tutor

Résumé bullet points:

   • <u>Initiated</u> the funding of entrepreneurial start-up by white knights who were members of investment clubs

MEASURE

(1)   appraise; assess; calculate; compute; determine; evaluate; gauge; mete; rate; quantify

Résumé bullet points:

   • <u>Measured</u> results of all advertising and promotion campaigns

MEDITATE

(1)   act as a go-between; arbitrate; intercede; intervene; judge; reconcile; referee; settle difference of opinion; umpire

Résumé bullet points:

- • <u>Mediated</u> disputes between union and nonunion workers

METHODIZE

(1)   order; organize; systematize

Résumé bullet points:

- • <u>Methodized</u> the reporting and evaluations of 250 value chain partners

ORGANIZE

(1)   arrange systematically; categorize; make arrangements, plans, or preparations for; order; put in order; sort out; systematize

(2)   control; coordinate; fix; manage; take charge

Résumé bullet points:

- • <u>Organized</u> work sharing operation, avoiding layoffs of 100 employees

PLAN

{also use in Problem Solving, Time Management, and HARD SKILLS: Time, Organizational, Planning and Time Management}

(1)   arrange; design; have in mind a project or purpose; intend; prepare; set up

(2)   arrange strategic ideas in diagrams, charts, sketches, graphs, tables, maps, and other documents

Résumé bullet points:

- • <u>Planned</u>, produced, and oversaw all vendor/exhibitor services at the industry's largest trade show

POSIT

{also use in Accountability, Attention to Detail, and HARD SKILLS: Analytical, Research, and Computational}

(1)   assume; conceive; conjecture; hypothesize; imagine; postulate; put forward; speculate; suggest; state or assume as fact; theorize

(1) Judy had first <u>posited</u> the possibility of a correlation between the variables.

QUANTIFY

{also use in Attention to Detail, HARD SKILLS: Accounting and Finance, and Analytical, Research, and Computational}

(1)   express something in quantifiable terms

(2)   numerical expression or explanation

(3)   determine or express or explain the quantity of, numerical measure of, or extent of

Résumé bullet points:

   • Quantified the results of needs gap analysis

RUMINATE

{also use in Communications and HARD SKILLS: Analytical, Research, and Computational}

(1)   chew over; cogitate; contemplate; mull over; ponder; reflect on; think over

(2)   mediate; turn over in one's mind

   (1), (2) Two dozen engineers ruminated over the plant's emission problems.

SATISFY

(1)   comply with; meet desires, expectations, needs; quench; satiate

(2)   fulfill needs and expectations, wishes, and desires

(3)   comply with the rules

Résumé bullet points:

   • Satisfied all requirements for IEEE certification

SCRUTINIZE

{also use in Communications}

(1)   analyze; examine carefully; dissect; inspect; pore over; search; study

Résumé bullet points:

   • Scrutinized vendor and supplier proposals for excessive prices

SIZE UP

(1)   form an opinion

(2)   take the measure of something

Résumé bullet points:

   • Sized up the operational requirements of foreign-made tool and die machines

CROSS-CULTURAL COMPETENCY

Cross-Cultural Competency is the ability to operate in different cultural settings.

ABERRATE

(1)   diverge or deviate from the straight path; diverge from the expected
Résumé bullet points:

- Aberrated from standard operating procedure (SOP) in cases that demanded field expediency

ABIDE

{also use in Accountability, Commitment and Dedication, Common Sense, Professional Demeanor and Presence, Reliability, Self-Manageable, and Work Ethic}

(1)   bear; continue; endure; go on being; put up with; stomach; take; tolerate

(2)   hold; remain; stand fast; stand for

(3)   remain with someone; stay

Collocates to: agreements, conditions, laws, norms, rules; resolutions, wishes

ABSORB

{also use in Accomplishments and Achievements, Accountability, Attention to Detail, Cognitive Load Management, Commitment and Detail, Common Sense, Flexibility, Learn, and Self-Manageable}

(1)   acquire; assimilate; attract; consume; digest; endure; engulf; fascinate; imbibe; soak up; sustain; take in; use up

(1) During the recent economic downturn, Boeing absorbed most of the price increases.

(2)   draw into oneself; grasp; realize; recognize; take in; understand

(3)   become captivated, interested, engaged, or preoccupied in; fascinated
Résumé bullet points:

- Absorbed the work of departments that have been eliminated, doubling my responsibilities

ACCEPT

{also use in Accountability, Cross-Cultural Competency, Take Direction, and Team Player}

(1)   admit; agree; believe; consent; say you will

(2) receive with gladness and approval

(3) receive; take something being offered

(4) bow to; endure; put up with; resign yourself to; tolerate

Résumé bullet points:

- Accepted the responsibilities for all my decisions

ACCLIMATE

{also use in Cognitive Load Management, Common Sense, Flexibility, Leadership, Learn, Novel and Adaptive Thinking, Professional Demeanor, Team Player, and Work Ethic}

(1) acclimatize; accustom yourself; adapt; adjust; become accustomed to a new environment or situation; familiarize; get used to

ACCOMMODATE

{also use in Accomplishments and Achievements, Compassion, Common Sense, Customer Awareness, Flexibility, and Outgoing}

(1) house; lodge; provide accommodations; put up

(2) adapt; be big enough for; contain; have capacity for; hold; reconcile; seat

(3) do a favor or a service for someone

(4) adjust; become accustomed; familiarize; get used to; make suitable

(5) allow for; assist; be of service; consider; find ways to help; oblige

Résumé bullet points:

- Accommodated the health, attire, and religious needs of all immigrant workers without a loss of team cohesiveness or productivity

ACQUAINT

{also use in Social Intelligence}

(1) accustom; aware; become familiar with; explain; inform; introduce; know; notify; present; run by; tell

(2) come to know personally

Résumé bullet points:

- Acquainted with proactive leadership and management styles

ADAPT

{also use in Accomplishments and Achievements, Attention to Detail, Commitment and Dedication, Common Sense, Creativity, Flexibility, Learn, and HARD SKILLS: Engineering and R&D}

(1)   acclimate; accommodate; adjust; change; conform; fashion; fit; get used to; make suitable; reconcile; square; suit; tailor

(2)   make fit, often by modification

(3)   cause something to change for the better
Résumé bullet points:

- <u>Adapted</u> working conditions to comply and exceed ADA requirements

ADJUST

{also use in Accountability, Common Sense, Engineering, R&D, Flexibility, and Work Ethic}

(1)   accommodate; alter; amend; attune; bend; change; correct; fine-tune; fix; modify; pacify; regulate; resolve; rectify; settle; tune-up; tweak
Résumé bullet points:

- <u>Adjusted</u> hours to accommodate mothers with infant child care issues

AID

(1)   abet; alleviate; assist; benefit; facilitate; give support to; help; minister to; serve; sustain; subsidize
Résumé bullet points:

- <u>Aided</u> workers with time off and reimbursement for fees for taking and passing English as a Second Language course.

ALLAY

{also use in Compassion}

(1)   alleviate; calm; dispel; put to rest; relieve; subside
Résumé bullet points:

- <u>Allayed</u> the fears of immigrant workers by hosting regular immigration rights workshops

ALLY

{also use in Outgoing and Social Intelligence}

(1)   align; associate; befriend; confederate; friend; help; league; join; support
Résumé bullet points:

- <u>Allied</u> with local businesses to create networking groups for immigrant workers

ASSIMILATE

(1)   absorb; accommodate; incorporate; standardize

Résumé bullet points:

- Assimilated quickly when transferred to our facility in Lima, Peru

AUGMENT

(1)   add to; boost; bump up; enlarge; expand; increase; supplement

Résumé bullet points:

- Augmented fulfillment positions with workers from sheltered workshops

BALANCE

{also use in Accountability, Attention to Detail, and Critical Thinking and Problem Solving}

(1)   assess; calculate; collate; compare; consider; evaluate; even out; equalize; keep upright; offset; settle; square; stabilize; stay poised; steady; tally; total; weigh; weight up

Résumé bullet points:

- Balanced the needs of workers with aggressive production objectives

BRANCH OUT

{also use in Risk Tolerant}

(1)   add new interests or new activities; begin doing new things

Résumé bullet points:

- Branched out in new endeavors

BROADEN

(1)   develop; enlarge; expand; extend; stretch; thicken; open up; widen

Résumé bullet points:

- Broadened the diversity of 1,000 employees by work-sharing and cross-training

COADJUTE

{also used in Team Player}

(1)   cooperate; work together

Résumé bullet points:

- Coadjuted worker disputes with one representative elected by worker votes

COALESCE

{also use in Accomplishments and Achievements, Accountability, Cognitive Load Management, Commitment and Dedication, Flexibility, Leadership, Learn, Social Intelligence, and Team Player}

(1)   blend; come together as one; combine; fuse or cause to grow together; join; merge; mingle; mix together different elements or parts; unite
Résumé bullet points:

- <u>Coalesced</u> organization's research into field leader

COLLABORATE

{also use in Accomplishments and Achievements, Commitment and Dedication, Cross-Cultural Competency, Self-Manageable, Take Direction, and Work Ethic}

(1)   act as a team; assist; cooperate; pool resources; team up; work jointly with; work together
Résumé bullet points:

- <u>Collaborated</u> with all union leaders to ensure company HR polices were in union contract specifications

CONSOLIDATE

{also use in Critical Thinking}

(1)   bring together; merge; strengthen; unite
Résumé bullet points:

- <u>Consolidated</u> five manufacturing and assembly operations into one location, making it more convenient for many workers and saving the company $2.5 million annually

CORRELATE

{also use in Attention to Detail and HARD SKILLS: Analytical, Research, and Computational}

(1)   associate; calculate or show the reciprocal relation between; come together; bring into mutual relation; correspond; parallel

(1) A person's race is weakly <u>correlated</u> with his eventual success in life.

DIVERSIFY

{also use in Flexibility and HARD SKILLS: Business and Business Sense}

(1)   branch out; expand; spread out; vary

Résumé bullet points:

- <u>Diversified</u> product selection for 2011 Winter Catalog, resulting in 10 percent increase in sales

EMBRACE

(1)   accept; include; involve; support; take on; welcome

(2)   clasp or hug in friendship, sociability, affection, or desire

(3)   contain; encircle; enclose; perceive to include; surround; take in mentally
Résumé bullet points:

- <u>Embraced</u> diversity as a hiring strategy

IMBRICATE

(1)   cover; overlap

(1) The emergency data center <u>imbricated</u> our in-house data center during the blackout.

UNIFY

{also use in Companionate and Intelligence}

(1)   blend; bring together; federate; merge; solidify; tie; unite
Résumé bullet points:

- <u>Unified</u> global workforce of 13,000 individuals

COMPUTATIONAL THINKING

Computational thinking is the ability to translate vast amounts of data into abstract concepts and to understand database reasoning.

AGGREGATE

{also use in Social Intelligence and HARD SKILLS: Administrative and Organizational}

(1)   accumulate; amass; collect; combine; gather together; sum; total; whole
Résumé bullet points:

- <u>Aggregated</u> all customer suggestions into topics for brainstorming sessions

ALLOCATE

(1)   allot; designate; devote; distribute

(2)   divide a sum of money or resources

Collocates to: for, funds, land, resources, quotas

Résumé bullet points:

- <u>Allocated</u> resources based on strategic value of the request

APPORTION

(1) allot; assign; divide and give out parts or shares according to a plan

Résumé bullet points:

- <u>Apportioned</u> interns to engineers based on work assignments

ARCHIVE

{also use in New Media Literature, Reliability}

(1) annals; collection; documentation; files; place or keep records in archive; library; store of data

Résumé bullet points:

- <u>Archived</u> project management scope statements

ASCRIBE

{also use in Accountability, Accuracy and Preciseness, Attention to Detail, Honesty and Integrity}

(1) accredit; arrogate; attribute something to someone; assert that something has been caused by someone or something

(1) The error was <u>ascribed</u> to a faulty chip.

Collocates to: attributes, meaning, motives, powers, tendencies, traits, qualities, values

ASSIGN

{also use in Accountability, Accuracy and Preciseness, and HARD SKILLS: Administrative and Organizational}

(1) allocate; allot; choose; consign; dispense; dole out; give; hand over; pick; select; transfer

(2) appoint; delegate; designate; detail; name

Résumé bullet points:

- <u>Assigned</u> student interns to departments

AUDIT

{also use in Accounting and Finance, Attention to Detail, and Design Mind-Set}

(1)   appraise; assess; check; count; examine; inspect; review; verify the accounting records of

Résumé bullet points:

   • Audited scope statements of projects with results documents

AUTOMATE

(1)   computerize; mechanize; program

Résumé bullet points:

   • Automated enrollment process, ensuring higher levels of student satisfaction

CALCULATE

{also use in Accountability, Accounting and Finance, and Engineering and R&D}

(1)   account; coax; compute; consider; deem; determine something; entice; enumerate; figure; persuade; rate

Résumé bullet points:

   • Calculated the cost of industrial sales calls

CLASSIFY

{also use in Attention to Detail and Gather Data and Convert into Information}

 (1)   arrange; assort; catalog; categorize; class; distribute into groups; grade; group; list by some order or sequence; organize; sort

Collocates to: advertising, as, by, documents, exposure, information

CODIFY

{also use in Gather Data and Convert into Information}

(1)   organize into a system of rules, codes, or principles to make clear and coherent

Résumé bullet points:

   • Codified rating system to rank the industry's more efficient logistics systems

COLLOCATE

(1)   arrange; catalog; set up
Résumé bullet points:

- Collocated formulas so common key terms could be found by internal search engine

COMPILE

{also use in Gather Data and Self-Manageable}

(1)   amass; assemble; collect and edit something; compose; gather and put together in an orderly form
Résumé bullet points:

- Compiled copies of project final deliverables for company library

CORRELATE

{also use in Attention to Detail, Cross-Cultural Competency, and HARD SKILLS: Analytical, Research, and Computational}

(1)   associate; bring into mutual relation; calculate or show the reciprocal relation between; come together; correspond; parallel

(1) The survey data indicated that the two factors were strongly correlated.

DATA MINE

{also use in New Media Literacy}

(1)   retrieval of facts and information from large databases
Résumé bullet points:

- Data mined for analysis online usage and customer interaction data using GM's preferred statistical package, SAS, and GM's preferred database software, Oracle SQL

DATA WAREHOUSE

(1)   store large data files for making business decisions
Résumé bullet points:

- Data warehoused using heterogeneous environment of super-sized Oracle clusters, regular databases, Amazon RDS nodes, and Amazon EC2-based map-reduce clusters

DATABASE

(1)   catalog; create information for storing; file; folder; list; record
Résumé bullet points:

- <u>Databased</u> all OSHA compliance claims

DIGITIZE

(1)   put content in digital form
Résumé bullet points:

- <u>Digitized</u> products and production

MODEL

(1)   archetype; design; facsimile; hold up as an example; mold; use an example to demonstrate meaning or prototype purpose; original; representation; standard
Résumé bullet points:

- <u>Modeled</u> all proposed marketing plans.

SORT

(1)   arrange on order by class or categories

(2)   place, arrange, or separate according to some class or category
Résumé bullet points:

- <u>Sorted</u> 14,000 customer files into 6 segmented markets.

TABULATE

{also use in Attention to Detail, HARD SKILLS: Accounting and Finance, and Analytical, Research, and Computational}

(1)   add up; chart; count; put facts in a table or column tally; total;
Résumé bullet points:

- <u>Tabulated</u> and summarized results of consumer panel discussions

CUSTOMER AWARENESS, ABLE TO DEAL WITH CUSTOMERS

Being customer aware means having empathy for customers and generally doing anything reasonable to satisfy customers' needs.

ACCEDE

{also use in Accountability, Commitment and Dedication, Flexibility, Outgoing, and Self-Manageable}

(1) agree; allow; approach; ascend; attain; come to; comply; conform; consent; enter upon; give assent; grant; succeed to; take over
Résumé bullet points:

• Acceded to subordinates' significantly higher levels of authority and responsibility in dealing with customers, thus improving customer service, retention, morale, and productivity

ACCOMMODATE

{also use in Accomplishments and Achievements, Common Sense, Compassionate, Cross-Cultural Competency, Flexibility and Outgoing}

(1) to house; lodge; provide accommodations; put up

(2) adapt; be big enough for; contain; have capacity for; hold; reconcile; seat

(3) do a favor or a service for someone

(4) adjust; become accustomed; familiarize; get used to; make suitable

(5) allow for; assist; be of service; consider; find ways to help; oblige
Résumé bullet points:

• Accommodated customers by customizing billing due dates

ACCREDITE

{also use in Accountability, Attention to Detail, Reliability, and HARD SKILLS: Administration and Organizational}

(1) approve; attribute; authorize; credit; endorse; recognize; sanction

(2) certify; supply with credentials or authority
Collocates to: colleges; courses, education, fully; ideas, institutions, programs, schools

ACQUIRE

{also use in Accomplishments, Design Mind-Set, Gather Data and Convert into Information, and Risk Tolerant}

(1)   attain; buy; come to possess; earn; gain; get; hold; obtain; purchase; receive

Résumé bullet points:

- <u>Acquired</u> and merged US Census data into customer database

ACTUATE

{also use in Accomplishments, Achievements, Attention to Detail and Accuracy, Creativity, Leadership, and Risk Tolerant}

(1)   activate; arouse to action; motivate; put into motion; start; trigger

Résumé bullet points:

- <u>Actuated</u> employees' sense of ownership by motivating them to do well by being good

ATTRACT

(1)   allure; appeal; captivate; charm; draw; enchant; fascinate; lure; magnetize; pull

Résumé bullet points:

- <u>Attracted</u> significantly higher numbers of customers to Web site with targeted email
- <u>Attracted</u> high-volume prospects with special promotions

BRING TOGETHER

(1)   cause to become joined or linked

(2)   bring together in a common cause or emotion

Résumé bullet points:

- <u>Brought together</u> vendors in regular strategic value chain planning
- <u>Brought together</u> the most talented thought leaders in the field

BUILD

{also use in Accountability and Research and R&D}

(1)   construct; erect; put up; raise; rear

(2)   grow; improve; increase

Résumé bullet points:

- <u>Built</u> added value to Cline firms by focusing on customer-centric approach
- <u>Built</u> and empowered award-winning cohesive teams that consistently achieved high standards of quality and productivity in completive markets

CARRY THE WATER

{also use in Commitment and Dedication, Leadership, Self-Confidence, and Work Ethic}

(1)   bear the main responsibility for something
Résumé bullet points:

- Carried the water for stronger customer initiatives

CULTIVATE

{also use in Commitment and Dedication, Customer Awareness, Intelligence, and Self-Manageable}

(1)   develop; encourage; foster; help; nurture; promote; refine; support to tend to; till; work on
Résumé bullet points:

- Cultivated repeat buyers with targeted marketing

SUPPORT

(1)   aid; encourage, help, or comfort

(2)   carry or bear the weight for; keep from falling, slipping, or dropping

(3   give approval; uphold
Résumé bullet points:

- Supported an ever-growing number of customers seeking cloud solutions

DESIGN MIND-SET

A design mind-set is the ability to develop tasks and work processes for the desired outcomes.

ACQUIRE

{also use in Accomplishments, Customer Awareness, Gather Data and Convert into Information, and Risk Tolerant}

(1)   attain; buy; come to possess; earn; gain; get; hold; obtain; purchase; receive
Résumé bullet points:

- Acquired training, knowledge, and experience to serve a project management team leader

ADD

(1)   add together; append; augment; combine; count up; enhance; summate; supplement; tally; tote up; join; unite

(2)   be logical; make sense

(3)   put figures together to make a total

(4)   complement; improve; increase

Résumé bullet points:

- Added four new customers, a new industry, and more than $1 million in revenue

ADHERE

{also use in Critical Thinking}

(1)   affix; bond; hold; hold fast; glutamate; remain; stick to something; stay

Résumé bullet points:

- Adhered to highest standards for quality

ADJUDICATE

[also use in Accountability, Cognitive Load Management, and Critical Thinking}

(1)   act as judge; listen; mediate; preside over argument; settle

Résumé bullet points:

- Adjudicated disputes between engineers over technical issues

ALIGN

{also use in Attention to Detail, Commitment and Dedication, Self-Manageable, and Social Intelligence}

(1)   ally; adjust; bring oneself into agreement with; correct; level; parallel; straighten

(2)   arrange something in reference to something else

Résumé bullet points:

- Aligned personal objectives with the objectives of the firm

AMEND

(1)   change for the better; correct; enhance; improve; modify; set right

Résumé bullet points:

- Amended field manuals to incorporate new standards

APPRAISE

(1)   estimate; determine worth of; give notice; inform; judge
Résumé bullet points:

  • <u>Appraised</u> the value of low-mileage luxury automobiles

APPRISE

(1)   acquaint; describe; enlighten; explain; impart; inform; notify; pass on; tell
Résumé bullet points:

  • <u>Apprised</u> customers of options of leasing versus buying

APPROVE

{also use in Accountability and Self-Manageable}

(1)   accept; agree to; attest; back up; command; commend; endorse; favor; praise; ratify; sanction; support

(2)   allow; authorize; consent; grant; pass; sanction
Résumé bullet points:

  • <u>Approved</u> all proposals to key accounts

ARRAY

{also use in Attention to Detail and HARD SKILLS: Analytical, Research, and Computational}

(1)   gamut; place in an orderly arrangement; set out for display or use

(2)   marshal troops; parade; place an order
<u>Collocates to: about, according, against, around, before, behind, in, on</u>

ASSERT

{also use in Analytical, Computational, and Research}

(1)   affirm; allege; aver; avow; claim; contend; declare; emphasize; protest; state strongly; stress

(2)   champion; defend; establish; insist upon; maintain; make a claim for; stand up for; support; uphold

  (1), (2)   The American HQ <u>asserted</u> authority over the European partner firm.

ASSESS

(1) estimate; impose; judge; value

(2) estimate the value, cost, benefit, or worth of
Résumé bullet points:

- Assessed the value of potential acquisitions

ASSEVERATE

{also use in Attention to Detail, Cognitive Load Management, and Communications}

(1) assert; aver; avouch; avow; declare earnestly or solemnly; hold; maintain

(1) He asseverated that the mistakes in the report would be corrected.

AUDIT

{also use in Accounting and Finance, Attention to Detail, and Computational Thinking}

(1) appraise; assess; check; count; examine; inspect; review; verify the accounting records of

Résumé bullet points:

- Audited Information Technology (IT) infrastructures, maintaining data integrity and operating effectively to achieve the organization's goals or objectives

AUTHENTICATE

(1) confirm; endorse; serve to prove; substantiate; validate
Résumé bullet points;

- Authenticated the sealed bids for auction items in excess of $25,000

BATCH PROCESS

{also use in New Media Literacy}

(1) process as a single unit or batch in automatic data processing
Résumé bullet points:

- Batch processed customer invoices

BATTLE TEST

(1) test something under the most difficult of conditions

(1) The cloud computing software was battle tested when our system failed in a blackout.

BENCHMARK

{also use in Attention to Detail, Learn, Professional Demeanor; HARD SKILLS: Advertising, Branding, PR, Sales, and Marketing; and HARD SKILLS: Business and Business Sense}

(1)   commence; identify and learn from the best business practices; level point of reference; standard; target
Résumé bullet points:

   • <u>Benchmarked</u> annual department results

BETA TEST

{also use in Leadership, Risk Tolerant, and HARD SKILLS: Analytical, Research, Computational}

(1)   field test; road test; sample prior to rollout
Résumé bullet points:

   • <u>Beta tested</u> all new versions of cloud software

BIFURCATE

(1)   branch; divide into sections; fork; split into two sections or pieces

   (1) The <u>bifurcated</u> analysis displayed the expected results.

BOLSTER

(1)   hold up; prop up; reinforce; support
Résumé bullet points:

   • <u>Bolstered</u> revenues and profits with constant development of aftermarket products and services

BOOKEND

(1)   bracket; enclose; precede and follow

   (1) The technology plan <u>bookended</u> our business plan covering today's needs as well as our projected needs into the next decade.

BOOTSTRAP

{also use in Common Sense and Self-Manageable}

(1)   initiate; manage without assistance; succeed with few resources
Résumé bullet points:

   • <u>Bootstrapped</u> new product development during economic downturn

BRING ABOUT

{also use in Commitment and Dedication}

(1) be the reason for; cause
Résumé bullet points:

- <u>Brought about</u> changes in outdated performance measurements

CATALOG OR CATALOGUE

(1) arrange; classify; list; put together; register
Résumé bullet points:

- <u>Cataloged</u> all design changes

CENTRALIZE

{also use in Attention to Detail and HARD SKILLS: Administrative and Organizational}

(1) consolidate; bring power of something to the central organization
Résumé bullet points:

- <u>Centralized</u> all regulatory reporting

CERTIFY

{also use in Attention to Detail, Honesty, and Integrity}

(1) assure; attest; confirm; testify; verify; vouch; witness
Résumé bullet points:

- <u>Certified</u> Cisco platform designer

CHART

(1) design; diagram; graph; graphic presentation; map; plan; plot; table; visual aid
(2) chronicle; follow; keep record of; log; monitor; outline; project; record; resister
Résumé bullet points:

- <u>Chartered</u> development of software simulation and modeling methods from vendors

CODE

(1)   systematic statement or instructions
Résumé bullet points:

  • <u>Coded</u> medical records, monitoring all government-related coding and
    billing practices, including NCD, LCD/LMRP, OCE and CCI edit man-
    agement, payment reconciliation, and financial impact analysis

COLLATE

{also use in Accomplishments and Achievements, Cogitative Load
Management, Team Player, and HARD SKILLS: Gather Data and Convert to
Information}

(1)   assemble or collect to compare; bring together; gather; pool; pull together
Résumé bullet points:

  • <u>Collated</u> binary search or half-interval search algorithms

CONFIGURE

(1)   align; design in particular way; set up in particular way
Résumé bullet points:

  • <u>Configured</u> multiple models of Cisco switches in a VLAN configuration

DEBUG

{also use in New Media Literacy}

(1)   clear up; correct; eliminate errors or malfunctions; fix; mend; repair;
      restore; service; sort out
Résumé bullet points:

  • <u>Debugged</u> department's software

DEFINE

{also use in Accomplishments and Achievements, Accountability, Accuracy
and Preciseness, Attention to Detail, Critical Thinking and Problem Solving}

(1)   characterize; classify; describe; determine or set down boundaries; distin-
      guish; identify; label; term

(2)   circumscribe; delimitate; delimit; demarcate; mark out
Résumé bullet points

  • <u>Defined</u> global budgeting, forecasting, revenue, and profitability objec-
    tives for 17 international business units

DELIMIT

{also use in Attention to Detail, Design Mind-Set, and Time Management}

(1)   define; demarcate; determine; fix boundaries; restrict; set limits; state clearly

(1) The study's results were also <u>delimited</u> to the specific instruments used.

<u>Collocates to: area, boundaries, carefully, clearly, spatially, within</u>

DEMARCATE

(1)   set boundaries; set mark; separate clearly
<u>Collocates to: area, by, border, boundaries, clearly, sharply, space</u>

DEPUTE

(1)   give authority to someone else to act as your agent or deputy
Résumé bullet points

- <u>Deputed</u> by CEO to perform some duties

DESIGNATE

(1)   call; circumscribe; choose; elect; entitle; identify; label; name; nominate; select; style; title

(2)   allocate; indicate; point out; specify
Résumé bullet point:

- <u>Designated</u> point person on design issues

DISENTANGLE

{also use in Cognitive Thinking and Self-Manageable}

(1)   clear; free from entanglements and ties; find solutions to problems; straighten out

(1) Her insights and negotiating skills <u>disentangled</u> the otherwise complicated situation.

IMBUE

(1)   indoctrinate; influence; inspire thoroughly; instill; pervade
Résumé bullet points:

- <u>Imbued</u> with the spirit of "just get it done"

OBSERVE

{also use in Gather Data and Convert into Information, Take Direction, and HARD SKILLS: Analytical, Research, and Computational}

(1)   examine; make a remark; monitor; notice; perceive; say; scrutinize; study; survey; view; watch attentively

(1) The marketplace was <u>observed</u> for signs of shifting consumer behavior.

ORCHESTRATE

{also use in Accountability and Attention to Detail}

(1)   combine and adapt to obtain a particular outcome

(2)   arrange or organize surreptitiously to achieve a desired effect
Résumé bullet points:

- <u>Orchestrated</u> companywide get-out-the-vote campaigns, including publicity, civics training, and transportation pools on election day

PERSEVERATE

{also use in Attention to Detail and Reliability}

(1)   continue something; repeat something insistently or over and over again
Résumé bullet point:

- <u>Perseverated</u> regardless of obstacles

PROJECT

{also use in HARD SKILLS: Accounting and Finance}

(1)   estimate; expect; forecast; plan; proposal; scheme

(2)   extend outward toward something else

(3)   cause a light shadow to fall on a surface

(4)   attribute an emotion to another person
Résumé bullet points:

- Managed a <u>project</u> involving designing a new toy that became top-selling product for four years

RATIOCINATE

{also use in Attitude and HARD SKILLS: Accounting and Finance}

(1)   work toward a solution through logical thinking and reason

(1) My <u>ratiocinated</u> approach helped a previously divided staff to accept the new policy as beneficial to the health of the firm and to their job security.

SOLVE

{also use in Accomplishments and Achievements, Creativity, and Accounting and Finance}

(1)   find a solution; settle

(2)   provide or find a suitable answer to a problem
Résumé bullet points:

- <u>Solved</u> many design problems

STOVE PIPE

{also use in HARD SKILLS: Business and Business Sense}

(1)   stack strategies, ideas, or plans
Résumé bullet points:

- <u>Stove piped</u> customer suggestions and ideas to have them ready to implement on short notice

STREAMLINE

(1)   make more efficient by employing faster or simpler working method

(2)   improve the efficiency or appearance of; modernize
Résumé bullet points:

- <u>Streamlined</u> accounts receivable system, improving cash flow

SYNCHRONIZE

(1)   be synchronous; direct a desired outcome; move or occur at the same time or rate

(1) The accounts team <u>synchronized</u> the sales, aftermarket activities, billing, warranty program, and follow-up service.

WHITE BOARD

(1)   brainstorm; get ideas down; list ideas and thoughts; strategize

(1) The marketing manager <u>white boarded</u> the brainstorming session.

DRIVE AND PASSION, TENACITY

Drive and passion are the motivation to work hard and excel.

ACCENTUATE

{also use in Accountability, Accuracy and Preciseness, Attention to Detail and Accuracy, Cognitive Load Management}

(1)   accent; emphasize; heighten; intensify

(1) My branding plan <u>accentuated</u> the product's unique benefits in a way that more people could relate.

(2)   play up; make more noticeable; stress something
<u>Collocates to: differences, opportunities, positives, shapes</u>

Résumé bullet points:

- <u>Accentuated</u> company's strategic objectives in the design and writing of the annual report, which won an award from the PR Association

ACCOMPLISH

{also use in Accomplishments and Achievements, Accountability, Accuracy and Precision, Attention to Detail, Leadership, Motivated, Novel and Adaptive Thinking, and Work Ethic}

(1)   achieve; attain; bring about; carry out; cause to happen; complete; do; gain; get done; finish; fulfill; make happen; make possible; produce; pull off; reach; realize; undertake

Résumé bullet points:

- <u>Accomplished</u> all stated goal on time and within budget

ACHIEVE

{also use in Accomplishments and Achievements, Attitude, Education, Leadership, Motivated, Novel and Adaptive Thinking, Risk Tolerant, and Self-Confidence}

(1)   accomplish; attain; complete; conclude; do; finish; get; perform; pull off; reach; realize

(2)   succeed in doing something

Résumé bullet points:

- <u>Achieved</u> the highest performance evaluation ratings

AMASS

{also use in Accomplishments and Achievements, Education, Motivated, and Self-Manageable}

(1)   accrue; accumulate; assemble; build up; collect; compile; gather together; hoard; pile up; store up

Résumé bullet points:

• <u>Amassed</u> 75 customer appreciation letters and recommendations

BATTLE

(1)   combat; competition; duel; encounter; fight; fracas; fray; melee; skirmish; wage a fight against

Résumé bullet points:

• <u>Battled</u> for market share

BROKE THROUGH

{also use in Risk Tolerant and Self-Manageable}

(1)   unexpected gain or improvement

(2)   new idea

Résumé bullet points:

• <u>Broke through</u> clutter of competition to lead

BUMP THE SHARK

{also use in Common Sense}

(1)   push back against an aggressive person; stand up against an intrusive or aggressive or assertive verbal assault

(1) In the past, Tom would have just sulked away, but today he <u>bumped the shark</u> and made Phil back down from his pompous position.

(2)   fight back against a bully

CHALLENGE

(1)   contest; deft; dare; went up against

(2)   goal; go through ordeal or trial of courage, strength, will, ideas; obstacle

Résumé bullet points:

• <u>Challenged</u> "this is the way it was always done" thinking

CHANNEL

(1) course; conduit; control; direct; feed; path; route

(2) concentrate; focus

Résumé bullet points:

- <u>Challenged</u> outmoded, obsolete methods and suggested progressive, empirical, tested approaches

CHIP AWAY

(1) break down big problems or issues into smaller components that are easier to work on

(2) remove or withdraw gradually

(1) The sales team <u>chipped away</u> at the competition's lead.

COMMAND

(1) bid; charge; direct; enjoin; instruct; lead; order; require; tell

Résumé bullet points:

- <u>Commanded</u> respect by my work ethic, dedication, and personal commitment

COMPETE

(1) content; contest; state of rivalry; match skills with someone

Résumé bullet points:

- <u>Competed</u> for top sales honors every year

CONDUCT

(1) carry on; control; direct; guide; head; lead; manage; operate; steer; supervise

Résumé bullet points:

- <u>Conducted</u> English as a second language courses for immigrant workers

CONTRIBUTE

{also use in Social Intelligence and Work Ethic}

(1) chip in; come across; come through; donate; exacerbate; give or supply in common with others; kick in; subscribe

Résumé bullet points:

- <u>Contributed</u> 20 percent of the annual sales revenues

CONVENE

(1) arrange; assemble; call; gather; organize; set up; summon
Résumé bullet points:

> • <u>Convened</u> an idea exchange of the industry's top thought leaders

DISENCUMBER

(1) free from burden, free something hindering; rid of something undesirable; unburden
Résumé bullet points:

> • <u>Disencumbered</u> marketing from the "push" mentality

DISTRIBUTE

(1) apportion; arrange; deal; dispense; divide; divvy; dole out; measure; parcel; portion; scatter; share; spread
Résumé bullet points:

> • <u>Distributed</u> workload among 20 engineers

EMPOWER

{also use in Accountability and Work Ethic}

(1) allow; authorize; give authority or power to; sanction

(2) make one stronger and more confident, especially in controlling his life and claiming his rights
Résumé bullet points:

> • <u>Empowered</u> all staff with authority and responsibility

EXCEED

{also use in Accomplishments and Achievements and Accountability}

(1) beat; go beyond; surpass what was expected or thought possible; be more or greater than; outdo
Résumé bullet points:

> • <u>Exceeded</u> expectations and quotas of all supervisors

EXCEL

{also use in Work Ethic}

(1) shine; stand out; surpass

(2)   be better, greater, or superior to others in the same field, profession, endeavor

Résumé bullet points:

- <u>Excelled</u> in foreign language skills; capable of speaking six languages fluently

EXECUTE

(1)   accomplish; carry out; carry into effect; finish; follow through; fulfill

(2)   create or produce in accordance with an idea or plan

(3)   perform as expected; run an instruction or program

Résumé bullet points:

- <u>Executed</u> all responsibilities and duties of a Rotary Fellowship winner

EXEMPLIFY

(1)   illustrate by example; serve or show as a good example

(2)   make a legally attested or certified copy or transcript of a document under seal

Résumé bullet points:

- <u>Exemplified</u> professionalism, honesty, and dependability in carrying out duties and responsibilities as treasurer, overseeing annual budget of $2.5 million

EXHORT

(1)   admonish strongly; encourage earnestly by advice or warning; insist; press; push; urge

Résumé bullet points:

- <u>Exhorted</u> team to work to their strengths

EXPEDIT

{also use in Accomplishments and Achievements and Time Management}

(1)   accelerate; hurry up; rush

(2)   speed up or make easy the process of or action of

(3)   dispatch; send off; issue officially

<u>Collocates to: process, shipping, timetables, treatment, trials</u>

Résumé bullet points:

- <u>Expedited</u> shipping services for customers

FAST-TRACK

{also use in Work Ethic and HARD SKILLS: Business and Business Sense}

(1)   bypass others; rapid; speed up
Résumé bullet points:

  • Fast-tracked market growth projects

INTERPOSE

{also use in Accountability}

(1)   aggressive; arbitrate; insert; intercept; interfere; intermediate; meddle;
      mediate; unsolicited opinion; offer assistance or presence; put between
Résumé bullet points:

  • Interposed an additional barrier between the host and the clients

LAUNCH

(1)   begin; commence; dispatch; embark; get underway; hurl; initial steps;
      introduce; release something; let loose something; send off; shoot; start or
      kick off something

(2)   introduce something; inaugurate; present; reveal; start marketing;
      unleash; unveil
Résumé bullet points:

  • Launched five new business start-ups.

MARSHAL

(1)   arrange; assemble; gather all resources to achieve a goal; mobilize;
      organize

(2)   put in delineated order
Résumé bullet points:

  • Marshaled 20-person, multidiscipline, cross-functional project
    management team

MAXIMIZE

{also use in Accomplishments and Achievements, Accounting and Finance,
and Accountability}

(1)   make best use of; make as great or as large as possible; raise to the high-
      est possible degree
Résumé bullet points:

  • Maximized merit bonus every year

MOTIVATE

{also use in Accountability, Accuracy and Preciseness, Attention to Detail, Commitment and Dedication, Communication, Creativity, Drive and Passion, Leadership, and Motivated}

(1)   cause; egg on; encourage; incentivize; induce; inspire; provide with a motive; prompt; provoke; stimulate; trigger

Résumé bullet points:
  • <u>Motivated</u> staff by focusing on their individual strengths

PIONEER

{also use in Accomplishments and Achievements, Creativity, Manageable, Motivated, and Self-Confidence}

(1)   first to develop new ideas or concepts; lead the way

Résumé bullet points:
  • <u>Pioneered</u> concept of using interns

WEIGH IN

(1)   argue; discuss; join in a cause; take part

(1) Our foreign subsidiary <u>weighed in</u> on the discussion to shift production back to the US.

ZERO IN

(1)   give full attention to something

(2)   aim directly at

Résumé bullet points:

  • <u>Zeroed in</u> on highest priority prospects

FLEXIBILITY, AVAILABILITY

Flexibility is the ability to make changes when the circumstances are right to manage business needs.

ABSORB

{also use in Accomplishments and Achievements, Accountability, Attention to Detail, Cognitive Load Management, Commitment and Detail, Common Sense, Cross-Cultural Competency, Learn, and Self-Manageable}

(1)   assimilate; acquire; attract; consume; digest; endure; engulf; fascinate; imbibe; sustain; soak up; take in; use up

(2)   draw into oneself; grasp; realize; recognize; take in; understand

(3)   become captivated, interested, engaged, or preoccupied in; fascinate

Résumé bullet points:

- Absorbed additional new department, including personnel, budget, and objectives, and led all managers in department productivity gains of prior year

ACCEDE

{also use in Accountability, Customer Awareness, Flexibility, Outgoing, and Self-Manageable}

(1)   agree; allow; approach; ascend; attain; come to; comply; conform; consent; enter upon; give assent; grant; succeed to; take over

(2)   enter upon an office

Résumé bullet points:

- Acceded to the post of president of industry trade association

ACCLIMATE

{also use in Cognitive Load Management, Common Sense, Cross-Cultural Competency, Leadership, Learn, Novel and Adaptive Thinking, Professional Demeanor, Team Player, and Work Ethic}

(1)   acclimatize; accustom yourself; adapt; adjust; become accustomed to a new environment or situation; familiarize; get used to

Résumé bullet points:

- Acclimated to new roles and responsibilities quickly

ACCOMMODATE

{also use in Accomplishments, Common Sense, Compassionate, Cross-Cultural Competency, Customer Awareness, Flexibility, and Outgoing}

(1)   house; lodge; provide accommodations; put up

(2)   adapt; be big enough for; contain; have capacity for; hold; reconcile; seat

(3)   do a favor or a service for someone

(4)   adjust; become accustomed; familiarize; get used to; make suitable

(5)   allow for; assist; be of service; consider; find ways to help; oblige

Collocates to: change, demand, desire, difference, growth, guest, need, request, passengers, schedule, space, special case(s), student

ACCUSTOM

{also use in Cross-Cultural Competency}

(1)   acclimatize to; acquaint; adapt; adjust to; attune to; familiarize; get to know; get used to; habitual; inure

(2)   become accustomed to

Résumé bullet points:

- Accustomed to new responsibilities in shortest possible time

ADAPT

{also use in Accomplishments and Achievements, Attention to Detail, Commitment and Dedication, Common Sense, Creativity, Cross-Cultural Competency, Learn, and HARD SKILLS: Engineering and R&D}

(1)   acclimate; accommodate; adjust; change; conform; fashion; fit; get used to; make suitable; reconcile; square; suit; tailor

(2)   make fit, often by modification

(3)   cause something to change for the better

Résumé bullet points:

- Adapted quickly to new routine of the management team from acquiring company

ADJUST

{also use in Accountability, Common Sense, Cross-Cultural Competency, Engineering, R&D, and Work Ethic}

(1)   accommodate; alter; amend; attune; bend; change; correct; fine-tune; fix; make change; modify; pacify; regulate; resolve; rectify; settle; tune up; tweak

Résumé bullet points:

- Adjusted to relocation

AGREE

{also use in Accountability and Polite}

(1)   accord; affirm; concur; consent; get together; grant; harmonize; jibe; match; say yes; square

Résumé bullet points:

- Agreed to serve as leader of new products development team

ALTERNATE

(1)   every other; in turns; rotate; swing; vary

(2)   exchange; serve as a substitute; swap

(3)   appear repetitively and regularly in a sequence with something else
Résumé bullet points:

- Alternated with another manager as building fire warden

ARBITRATE

{also use in Critical Thinking}

(1)   adjudicate; decide; intercede; judge; mediate; negotiate; pass judgment;
      referee; settle; sort out
Résumé bullet points:

- Arbitrated disputes between businesses and customers

COALESCE

{also use in Accountability, Accomplishments and Achievements, Cognitive
Load Management, Commitment and Dedication, Cross-Cultural Competency,
Leadership, Learn, Social Intelligence, and Team Player}

(1)   come together as one; combine; grow together; join; unite
Collocates to: around, groups, to, with

CONCUR

(1)   act together; agree; be of the same opinion; coincide; come to agreement
      with others

   (1) The majority of the members concurred with the president's remarks.

DIVERSIFY

{also use in Cross-Cultural Competency and HARD SKILLS: Business and
Business Sense}

(1)   branch out; expand; spread out; vary
Résumé bullet points:

- Diversified the staff

NEGOTIATE

(1)   bargain; confer, reach agreement by discussion or compromise
Résumé bullet points:

  • <u>Negotiated</u> multimillion dollar contracts

HONESTY AND INTEGRITY

Honesty and integrity describe one's conscious act to consistently do what is legal, ethical, and morally correct.

ACKNOWLEDGE

{also use in Accountability, Learn, Outgoing, Professional Demeanor, and Self-Manageable}

(1)   admit; allow; avow; concede; confess; fess up; grant; own up; recognize

(2)   answer; react; reply; respond; return

(3)   greet; nod to; salute; wave to
Résumé bullet points:

  • <u>Acknowledged</u> by industry association as one of the field's Top 50
    Thought Leaders

AFFIRM

{also use in Accountability, Attention to Detail and Accuracy, Critical Thinking and Problem Solving}

(1)   acknowledge; affirm; announce; assert; asseverate; avow; confirm; establish; insist; pronounce; state; validate; verify

(2)   encourage; support; sustain; uphold
Résumé bullet points:

  • <u>Affirmed</u> the strategic objectives of the investors

ASCRIBE

{also use in Accountability, Accuracy and Preciseness, Attention to Detail, Computational Thinking}

(1)   accredit; arrogate; assert that something has been caused by someone or
    something; attribute something to someone
<u>Collocates to: attributes, meaning, motives, powers, qualities, tendencies, traits,
values</u>

ASSURE

(1)   comfort; convince; declare; ensure; give surety; guarantee; pledge; promise; reassure; swear

(2)   confirm; know for sure; nail down; substantiate; verify

Résumé bullet points:

- <u>Assured</u> intellectual property legal compliance of all software program purchases

ATTEST

{also use in Communications}

(1)   certify or witness or swear to

(1) The product claims were <u>attested</u> to by three independent sources.

AVER

{also use in Attention to Detail and Critical Thinking and Problem Solving}

(1)   affirm; assert the truthfulness of something; avow; claim; declare; maintain; profess; state; swear

Résumé bullet points:

- <u>Averred</u> all technological claims in firm's marketing and promotional materials

CERTIFY

{also use in Attention to Detail, Design Mind-Set, and Reliability}

(1)   assure; attest; confirm; testify; verify; vouch; witness

(1) The team <u>certified</u> that the project was complete.

FACTOR

(1)   aspect; cause; issue; make a part; make a reason

(2)   sell accounts receivables to obtain cash before the due date on the account

Résumé bullet points:

- <u>Factored</u> receivables as stopgap measure to obtain needed cash

FREELANCE

(1)   work in an unstructured manner without the processes and resources of an employer; work not as an employee

Résumé bullet points:

- <u>Freelanced</u> as a photographer

GARNER

(1)   accumulate; acquire; assemble; bring together; bunch up; collect; gain; gather; get; harvest; heap; earn; reap

Résumé bullet points:

- <u>Garnered</u> support of Board of Directors for strategic decisions

INTELLIGENCE

Intelligence is generally associated with knowledge, abstract thought, understanding, self-awareness, communication, reasoning, learning, having emotional knowledge, retaining, planning, and problem solving.

ABSTRACT

{also use in Cognitive Load Management}

(1)   detach; draw away from; extract; remove; select; separate; take out

(2)   abridge; condense; pr[ac]ecis; shorten; take or extract the relevant or important information from; purloin; synopsize; summarize

<u>Collocates to: context, data, information, knowledge, manner, social</u>

CEREBRATE

(ser´ ə brāt´)

{also use in Learn and Professional Demeanor}

(1)   consider; ponder; think; use one's power of mind

Résumé bullet points:

- <u>Cerebrated</u> with industry thought leaders and top management on strategic issues

CULTIVATE

{also use in Commitment and Dedication, Customer Awareness, Self-Manageable, and Social Intelligence}

(1)   develop; encourage; foster; help; nurture; promote; refine; support

(2)   tend to; till; work on

Résumé bullet points:

- <u>Cultivated</u> network of thought leaders to bounce ideas off

DELVE

{also use in Learn}

(1)   dig; examine; explore; inquire; investigate; look into; research; search

(2)   dip into; dive; hunt; plunge; reach; rummage

Résumé bullet points:

- <u>Delved</u> into new technologies

DISCOVER

{also use in Accomplishments and Achievements, Common Sense, Critical Thinking and Problem Solving, and Gather Data and Convert into Information}

(1)   ascertain; be first to learn something; determine; expose; find out; hear; learn; realize, see, or uncover something

Résumé bullet points:

- <u>Discovered</u> new applications for products

EDIFY

{also use in Cognitive Load Management, Communications, Compassionate, Learn, and Social Intelligence}

(1)   educate; enlighten; illuminate; improve; inform; instruct; teach

(2)   uplift morally, spiritually, or intellectually

(1), (2) The retreat program <u>edified</u> all who attended.

EDUCATE

{also use in Attention to Detail, Communications, and Learn}

(1)   discipline; edify; impart knowledge; inform; instruct; mentor; teach; train; tutor

(2)   develop and train the innate capacities of by schooling or education

(3)   provide knowledge in a particular area

Résumé bullet points:

- <u>Educated</u> team so they knew as much as me as about our business

EDUCE

{also use in Attention to Detail, Cognitive Load Management, Critical Thinking, and Leadership}

(1) come to conclusion; derive; evoke; solve a problem based on thoughtful consideration of facts

(1) The consulting team <u>deduced</u> from their observations that the firm needed to build its brand.

(2) deduce; draw out; elicit; infer

(3) bring out or develop; elicit from

IMBIBE

{also use in Cogitative Load Management and Learn}

(1) receive in the mind and retain; soak; steep; take in

(1) Repetition advertising <u>imbibed</u> viewers with slogans, jingles, and themes that were supposed to come into their attention unexpectedly.

INTERPRET

{also use in Attention to Detail}

(1) construe; explain; present in understandable terms; represent the terms of individual belief or judgment; tell the meaning of

Résumé bullet points:

• <u>Interpreted</u> the impact of all proposed new Federal regulations on the business giving the strategic planning group advanced planning time, thus keeping us ahead of the competition

LEADERSHIP AND MANAGEMENT

Leadership is the ability to use personal influence to get others to aid and support the achievement of a commonly agreed-upon task and to set priorities.

ACCLIMATE

{also use in Cognitive Load Management, Common Sense, Cross-Cultural Competency, Flexibility, Learn, Novel and Adaptive Thinking, Professional Demeanor, Team Player, and Work Ethic}

(1) acclimatize; accustom yourself; adapt; adjust; become accustomed to a new environment or situation; familiarize; get used to

(1) It took longer than he thought to become <u>acclimated</u> to New York City social life.

Résumé bullet points:

• <u>Acclimated</u> to leadership role quickly

ACCOMPLISH

{also use in Accomplishments and Achievements, Accountability, Accuracy and Precision, Attention to Detail, Drive, Passion and Tenacity, Motivated, Novel and Adaptive Thinking, and Work Ethic}

(1) achieve; attain; bring about; carry out; cause to happen; complete; do; gain; get done; finish; fulfill; make happen; make possible; produce; pull off; reach; realize; undertake

(1) The project team <u>accomplished</u> their first milestone on schedule.

Résumé bullet points:

- <u>Accomplished</u> all assigned goals and objectives

ACHIEVE

{also use in Accomplishments and Achievements, Attitude, Education, Leadership, Motivated, Novel and Adaptive Thinking, Risk Tolerant, and Self-Confidence}

(1) accomplish; attain; complete; conclude; do; finish; get; reach; perform; pull off; realize

(1) The firm <u>achieved</u> greater success when it began hiring more quali-fied candidates.

(2) succeed in doing something

Résumé bullet points:

- <u>Achieved</u> highest ratings possible for leadership in employee surveys of job satisfaction

ACT

{also use in Risk Tolerant and Self-Manageable}

(1) accomplish; acquit yourself; be active; behave; do something; take action; take steps; operate; proceed; react; respond; work

(2) act out; appear in; feign; impersonate; mock; perform; play in; pretend; simulate

Résumé bullet points:

- <u>Acted</u> as interim store manager during search for new manager

ACTUALIZE

(ak´c/hoo əl îz´)

(1) make real or actual; realize

(2)   fulfill the potential of

Résumé bullet points:

- <u>Actualized</u> the theory and concepts of Transformational Leadership

ACTUATE

{also use in Accomplishments, Attention to Detail, Creativity, Customer Awareness, and Risk Tolerant}

(1)   activate; arouse to action; motivate; put into motion; start; trigger

   (1) Toni's speech <u>actuated</u> the congress to finally act on the bill.

<u>Collocated with: controlled, hydraulically pneumatically, series, valves</u>

Résumé bullet points:

- <u>Actuated</u> employees to do well by being good

ADDUCE

(ə doo- ´s´)

(1)   allege; bring forward; cite as evidence; lead to; present; put forward

Résumé bullet points:

- <u>Adduced</u> evidence by results that leadership can be conditional and situational

ADUMBRATE

{also use in Cognitive Load Management and Risk Tolerant}

(1)   foreshadow; give a general description of something but not the details; obscure; overshadow; predict; prefigure; presage; summarize

Résumé bullet points:

- <u>Adumbrated</u> the principle that in a free market anyone can succeed

AMELIORATE

(ə mēl´y ərāt´)

{also use in Accomplishments and Achievements, Accountability. Accuracy and Preciseness, Attention to Detail, Creativity, Learn, Novel and Adaptive Thinking, and Self-Manageable}

(1)   correct a mistake; improve; make better; tolerate

   (1) Phillip <u>ameliorated</u> the issues in the business plan prior to the meeting with the investors.

(2)   correct a deficiency or defect; make right a wrong; take action that makes up for one's negative or improper actions

Résumé bullet points:

• Ameliorated the situation in which field sales had no input to marketing's lead generation program

ANALYZE

(an´ əlīz´)

(1)   consider; dissect; evaluate; examine; explore; interpret; investigate; probe; question; scrutinize; study

(1) Randi analyzed the situation from all positions before making her decision.

Collocates to: analysis, data, findings, results, sample, study

Résumé bullet points:

• Analyzed more data, from a larger more diverse range of sources, in the shortest time possible

APPERTAIN

(ap´ ər tān´)

(1)   apply; an attribute of; be appropriate; be part of; belong; relate to

(1) The importance of good communication skills appertains today as it did 200 years ago.

ASCERTAIN

(as´ ər tān´)

(1)   determine; discover; establish; find out; learn; realize; uncover

(1) He ascertained the problems by careful observation.

(2)   find out with certainty

Collocates to: definitely, easily, facts, fully, having

Résumé bullet points:

• Ascertained validity of worker's claims of unfair practices by supervisors

ASSIMILATE

(1)   absorb; accommodate; incorporate; standardize

Collocates to: easily, gradually, readily, thoroughly

Résumé bullet points:

- <u>Assimilated</u> the lessons learned working with veteran managers.

AUTHENTICATE

(1) confirm; endorse; serve to prove; substantiate; validate
Résumé bullet points:

- <u>Authenticated</u> documents sent by foreign investors

BETA TEST

{also use in Design Mind-Set, Risk Tolerant, and HARD SKILLS: Analytical, Research, Computational}

(1) field test; road test; sample prior to rollout
Résumé bullet points:

- <u>Beta tested</u> only products that met my strict functionality tests

CARRY THE WATER

{also use in Commitment, Dedication, Self-Confidence, and Work Ethic}

(1) bear the main responsibility for something
Résumé bullet points:

- <u>Carried the water</u> for employee benefits

CHAMPION

{also use in Accountability, Commitment and Dedication, Novel and Adaptive Thinking, and Self-Confidence}

(1) advocate; back; be a winner; campaign for; crusade for; excel; fight for; stand up for; support; uphold
Résumé bullet points:

- <u>Championed</u> the project team members who demonstrated creativity, innovation, and courage

COALESCE

{also use in Accountability, Accomplishments and Achievements, Commitment and Dedication, Cognitive Load Management, Cross-Cultural Competency, Flexibility, Learn, Social Intelligence, and Team Player}

(1) combine; come together as one; grow together; join; unite
<u>Collocated with: around, became, finally, formally into</u>

Résumé bullet points:

- <u>Coalesced</u> geographically diverse collection of 11 individuals into a strong unified team

COLLECT

(1)   arrange; catalog; gather; set up

Résumé bullet points:

- <u>Collected</u> and analyzed data

COMPARE

(1)   collate; contrast; exchange thoughts or ideas about something

Résumé bullet points:

- <u>Compared</u> favorably to others who had faced similar situations

CONCEPTUALIZE

{also use in Cognitive Load Management, Communications, and Learn}

(1)   create an understandable point out of a concept; interpret something from the abstract

(1) She took on the project and <u>conceptualized</u> the whole thing before committing it to paper.

<u>Collocated with: approach, experience, perception, theories</u>

Résumé bullet points:

- <u>Conceptualized</u> the idea that leadership is situational and conditional

CONVOKE

(1)   assemble; call together; convene; summon to a meeting

<u>Collocated with: assembly, congress, groups, meeting, officials, people</u>

Résumé bullet points:

- <u>Convoked</u> panels of thought leaders

CULL

(1)   amass; collect; gather; choose; glean; pick out; select

(1) The new sales manager <u>culled</u> out the weaker performers.

Résumé bullet points:

- <u>Culled</u> vendors and suppliers who did not fit into value chain relationship

EDUCE

{also use in Attention to Detail and Accuracy, Cognitive Load Management, Critical Thinking and Problem Solving, and Intelligence}

(1) come to conclusion; solve a problem based on thoughtful consideration of facts; derive; evoke

(1) They <u>educed</u> that the world was not flat.

(2) deduce; draw out; elicit; infer

(3) bring out or develop

Collocated with: change, evidence, facts, good, order, reason

Résumé bullet points:

• <u>Educed</u> the need to search internally for job candidates

EMEND

(1) correct or edit; remove faults in a scholarly or literary work; improve

(1) Our auditor <u>emended</u> the forms that incorrectly listed us an LLC.

(2) make scholarly corrections in a text

ENHANCE

{also use in Accomplishments and Achievements and Motivated}

(1) add to; augment; boost; develop; endow with beauty and elegance; grace

(2) improve the quality or condition of

(3) digitally or electronically improve the quality, tone, pitch, image of photos, recordings

Résumé bullet points:

• <u>Enhanced</u> the efficiency and effectiveness of in-house training

FACILITATE PROBLEM-SOLVING MEETINGS

(1) facilitate, lead, manage, supervise meetings focused on problem-solving agenda

Résumé bullet points:

• <u>Facilitated problem-solving meetings</u> that led to numerous ideas that were adopted

GALVANIZE

{also use in Critical Thinking and Social Intelligence}

(1)   activate; propel someone or something into sudden action; stimulate

(1) The FDC's action <u>galvanized</u> the drug industry to form a PAC to lobby against the rules.

INCENTIVIZE

(1)   encourage; provide one with a reason to work harder; provide with an incentive

Résumé bullet points:

- <u>Incentivized</u> employees to continue education with full tuition reimbursement program

LAUNCH

(1)   begin; commence; dispatch; embark; get underway; hurl; introduce; initial steps; launch release something; let loose something; send off; shoot; start or kick off something

(2)   introduce something; inaugurate; reveal; present; start marketing; unleash; unveil

Résumé bullet points:

- <u>Launched</u> successful direct mail campaigns in months the experts said are not good for mail campaigns

LEVERAGE

(1)   control; force; influence; power; pull; weight

Résumé bullet points:

- <u>Leveraged</u> employees' strengths

MANAGE

(1)   be in charge; handle effectively; watch and direct

(2)   achieve something; be successful

(3)   carry or function

Résumé bullet points:

- <u>Managed</u> multiple assignments, tasks, and responsibilities

MILITATE

(1)   have a substantial effect on; weigh heavily on

    (1) The sales team <u>militated</u> against altering the compensation plan.

REVAMP

(1)   determine training needs; reevaluate
Résumé bullet points:

    • <u>Revamped</u> product training

START

(1)   activate; begin; initiate; open up

(2)   jump, leap, or jerk in a startled way; make a sudden, involuntary, unexpected movement as if surprised
Résumé bullet points:

    • <u>Started</u> intuitional investment consultancy for not-for-profit organizations

    • <u>Started</u> small business value chain referral service connecting new business owners with vendors and suppliers seeking to specialize in value chain relationships

SYSTEMATIZE

(1)   organize; prioritize; put in place some organized and written plan
Résumé bullet points:

    • <u>Systematized</u> common sense into firm's policies

TOOK CHARGE

(1)   assume command or management; assume control over others; step up when needed
Résumé bullet points:

    • <u>Took charge</u> in crisis situations

TROUBLESHOOT

(1)   investigate and determine why things did not go according to plan; look into cause of problems
Résumé bullet points:

    • <u>Troubleshot</u> issues arising out of mergers and acquisitions, takeovers, and downsizing

UNIFY

{also use in Compassionate and Cross-Cultural Competency}

(1)   blend; bring together; federate; merge; tie; solidify; unite
Résumé bullet points:

- <u>Unified</u> the parts of the value chain

WALK THE WALK

(1)   actually doing what one says or promises regardless of the consequences
or cost

(1)   Our mangers <u>walked the walk</u> for their employees.

LEARN, GROW, TEACHABLE, WILLINGNESS TO LEARN

Learning is the willingness and ability to acquire new or modify existing
knowledge, behaviors, skills, values, or preferences.

ABET

{also use in Accountability, Commitment and Dedication, Motivated, and
Social Intelligence}

(1)   advocate; assist; back; back up; encourage; espouse; foment; help incite;
put up to; sanction; support; urge (especially in wrongdoing)
Résumé bullet points:

- <u>Abetted</u> the decision to expand globally

ABSORB

{also use in Accomplishments and Achievements, Accountability, Attention to
Detail, Cognitive Load Management, Common Sense, Commitment and
Detail, Cross-Cultural Competency, Flexibility, Learn, and Self-Manageable}

(1)   acquire; assimilate; attract; consume; digest; endure; engulf; fascinate;
imbibe; inure; sustain; soak up; take in; use up

(2)   draw into oneself; grasp; realize; recognize; take in; understand

(3)   become captivated, interested, engaged, or preoccupied in; fascinate
Résumé bullet points:

- <u>Absorbed</u> many new products into line

ACCLIMATE

{also use in Cognitive Load Management, Common Sense, Cross-Cultural Competency, Flexibility, Leadership, Learn, Novel Adaptive Thinking, Team Player, and Work Ethic}

(1)   acclimatize; adapt; accustom yourself; adjust; become accustomed to a new environment or situation; familiarize; get used to

Résumé bullet points:

• <u>Acclimated</u> easily to most situations

ACCLIMATIZE

(1)   acclimate; adapt; adjust; become accustomed; get used to; familiarize

(1) The repair team <u>acclimatized</u> before being transported to the South Pole to do repair work.

ACKNOWLEDGE

{also use in Accountability, Honesty, Integrity, Outgoing, Professional Demeanor, and Self-Manageable}

(1)   accept something as fact or truth; admit; allow; avow; concede; confess; fess up; grant; own up; recognize

(2)   answer; react; reply; respond; return

Résumé bullet points:

• <u>Acknowledged</u> thought leader in business planning

ADAPT

{also use in Accomplishments and Achievements, Attention to Detail, Commitment and Dedication, Common Sense, Creativity, Cross-Cultural Competency, and Flexibility}

(1)   acclimate; accommodate; adjust; change; conform; fashion; fit; get used to; make suitable; reconcile; square; suit; tailor

(1) Sandra <u>adapted</u> to her new role quicker than she expected.

(2)   make fit, often by modification

(3)   cause something to change for the better

Résumé bullet points:

• <u>Adapted</u> to serve under many different leadership styles

AMELIORATE

{also use in Accomplishments and Achievements, Accountability, Accuracy and Preciseness, Attention to Detail, Creativity, Leadership, Novel and Adaptive Thinking, and Self-Manageable}

(1)   correct a mistake; improve; make better; tolerate

(2)   correct a deficiency or defect; make right a wrong; take action that makes up for one's negative or improper actions

(2) The new manual ameliorated for the omission of how to make field repairs.

BENCHMARK

{also use in Attention to Detail, Design Mind-Set, Learn, Professional Demeanor; HARD SKILLS: Advertising, Branding, PR, Sales, and Marketing; HARD SKILLS: Business and Business Sense}

(1)   commence; identify and learn from the best business practices; level point of reference; standard; target

Résumé bullet points:

• Benchmarked specifications for systems implementation

CEREBRATE

(ser´ ə brāt´)

{also use in Intelligence and Professional Demeanor}

(1)   consider; ponder; think; use one's power of mind

Résumé bullet points:

• Cerebrated with industry thought leaders and top management on strategic issues

COALESCE

{also use in Accomplishments and Achievements, Accountability, Cognitive Load Management, Commitment and Dedication, Cross-Cultural Competency, Flexibility, Leadership, Social Intelligence, and Team Player}

(1)   come together as one; combine; grow together; join; unite

(1) The project management team eventually coalesced around the objectives.

CONCEPTUALIZE

{also use in Cognitive Load Management, Communications, and Leadership}

(1)   create an understandable point out of a concept; interpret something from the abstract

Résumé bullet points:

  • Conceptualized the connection of 27 locations by an intranet

CONCILIATE

{also use in Outgoing and Politeness}

(1)   appease; gain the regard or goodwill by good acts; pacify; reconcile; soothe the anger of; win over

  (1) They conciliated rather than sought a settlement.

DEDUCE

{also use in Attention to Detail and Critical Thinking and Problem Solving}

(1)   assume; conclude from evidence; conjecture; figure out; hypothesize; infer; posit; presume; reason; suppose; surmise; suspect; work out

  (1) The consulting team deduced from its observations that the firm needed to build brand.

(2)   trace the course of deviation

DELVE

{also use in Intelligence}

(1)   dig; examine; explore; inquire; investigate; look into; research; search

(2)   dip into; dive; hunt; plunge; reach; rummage

Résumé bullet points:

  • Delved into the use of new technologies

EDIFY

{also use in Cognitive Load Management, Communications, Compassionate, Intelligence, and Social Intelligence}

(1)   educate; enlighten; illuminate; improve; inform; instruct; teach

(2)   uplift morally, spiritually, or intellectually

  (1), (2) The speaker's message edified and raised the spirits of everyone in attendance.

EDUCATE

{also use in Attention to Detail, Communications, and Intelligence}

(1) discipline; edify; inform; impart knowledge; instruct; mentor; teach; train; tutor

(2) develop and train the innate capacities of by schooling or education

(3) provide knowledge in a particular area

Résumé bullet points:

  • Educated the public about nonprofit's earn revenues

EFFECTUATE

{also use in Accuracy and Preciseness and Commitment and Dedication}

(1) bring about; cause or accomplish something; effect

Collocates to: change, goals, intent, necessity, plans, policy, purpose, resources, standards

IMBIBE

{also use in Cognitive Load Management and Intelligence}

 (1) receive in the mind and retain; soak; steep; take in

  (1) Repetition advertising imbibed viewers with slogans, jingles, and themes that were supposed to come into their attention unexpectedly.

INSORB

{also use in Social Intelligence}

(1) absorb; incorporate; take in

Résumé bullet point:

  • Insorbed multidisciplinary knowledge

PERCEIVE

(1) become aware or conscious of through the senses; distinguish; identify; make out; notice; pick out; regard as

(2) notice; observe; remark; see; take in

(3) comprehend; feel; realize; sense

Résumé bullet points:

  • Perceived to be a thought leader

MOTIVATED

Motivated is to have or give the ability to do something in a more enthusiastic, interested, and committed way.

ABET

{also use in Accountability, Commitment and Dedication, Learn, and Social Intelligence}

(1) advocate; assist; back; back up; encourage; espouse; foment; help incite; put up to; sanction; support; urge (especially in wrongdoing)

Résumé bullet points:

• <u>Abetted</u> the decision to expand globally

ACCELERATE

{also use in Accomplishments and Achievements, Commitment and Dedication, Motivated, Self-Manageable, and HARD SKILLS: Time and Organizational Management}

(1) gather speed; go faster; grow; hurry; increase speed of; pick up the pace; speed up; quicken; rush

(2) cause to occur sooner

Résumé bullet points:

• <u>Accelerated</u> revenues to bottom-line profits

ACCOMPLISH

{also use in Accomplishments and Achievements, Accountability, Accuracy and Precision, Attention to Detail, Drive, Leadership, Novel and Adaptive Thinking, Passion and Tenacity, and Work Ethic}

(1) achieve; attain; bring about; carry out; cause to happen; complete; do; gain; get done; finish; fulfill; make happen; make possible; produce; pull off; reach; realize; undertake

Résumé bullet points:

• <u>Accomplished</u> shift from small regional to global business

ACHIEVE

{also use in Accomplishments and Achievements, Attitude, Drive and Passion, Education, Leadership, Novel and Adaptive Thinking, Risk Tolerant, and Self-Confidence}

(1) accomplish; attain; complete; conclude; do; finish; get; perform; pull off; reach; realize

(2)   succeed in doing something
Résumé bullet points:

   • <u>Achieved</u> 30 percent market share in highly competitive industry

ACTUALIZE

{also use in Accomplishments and Achievements, Attention to Detail, Common Sense, and Novel and Adaptive Thinking}

(1)   make real or actual; realize

(2)   fulfill the potential of
Résumé bullet points:

   • <u>Actualized</u> virtual transactions, giving customers a human contact

AMASS

{also use in Accomplishments and Achievements, Drive and Passion, Education, and Self-Manageable}

(1)   accrue; accumulate; assemble; build up; collect; compile; collect; gather together; hoard; pile up; store up
Résumé bullet points:

   • <u>Amassed</u> 75 customer appreciation letters and recommendations

BLUE SKY

{also use in Cognitive Load Management and Communication}

(1)   visionary thinking; out-of-the-box strategic long-range thinking
Résumé bullet points:

   • <u>Blue skied</u> strategic long-term strategy

CAJOLE

{also use in Communication}

(1)   blandish; coax; entice; flatter; inveigle; soft-soap; sweet-talk; wheedle
Résumé bullet points:

   • <u>Cajoled</u> when necessary

CARRY THROUGH

{also use in Reliability, Team Player, and Work Ethic}

(1)   persist; put into action; take the most difficult

Résumé bullet points:

- <u>Carried through</u> on promises and plans

CRUSADE

{also use in Risk Tolerant and Self-Confident)

(1) adopt a cause or mission with great enthusiasm and motivation; campaign for which one has placed a high priority; emotional drive to achieve something; take risk or stakes

(1) Many volunteers <u>crusaded</u> for their causes.

ENERGIZE

(1) boost; give energy; invigorate; strengthen
Résumé bullet points:

- <u>Energized</u> those around me

ENHANCE

{also use in Accomplishment and Achievements and Leadership}

(1) add to; augment; boost; develop; endow with beauty and elegance; grace

(2) improve the quality or condition of

(3) digitally or electronically improve the quality, tone, pitch, image of photos, recordings
Résumé bullet points:

- <u>Enhanced</u> processes, procedures, and controls of Accounting and Finance Division

INVOKE

(1) appeal to; bring up; call up; call upon; compel observance; enforce; pray to; raise; recall; remember

(2) bring into play; bring up; cite; quote; state; use

(3) call up; conjure up; evoke; make reference to; refer to; remind of
Résumé bullet points:

- <u>Invoked</u> proactive callbacks of products to protect the brand and customer relations

MOBILIZE

(1)   activate; assemble; call up; drum up support for; gather people and resources for something; generate support for something; marshal; muster; organize; rally

Résumé bullet points:

- Mobilized industry resources to campaign against anti-online bullying

MOTIVATE

{also use in Accountability, Accuracy and Preciseness, Attention to Detail, Commitment and Dedication, Communication, Creativity, Drive and Passion, and Leadership}

(1)   cause; egg on; encourage; incentivize; induce; inspire; prompt; provide with a motive; provoke; stimulate; trigger

Résumé bullet points:

- Motivated people to achieve their best

OVERACHIEVE

{also use in Work Ethic}

(1)   do or perform better than expected

Résumé bullet points:

- Overachieved on most tasks

PIONEER

{also use in Accomplishments and Achievements, Creativity, Drive, Manageable, Motivated, Passion, Self-Confidence, and Tenacity}

(1)   be the first to develop new ideas or concepts; lead the way

Résumé bullet points:

- Pioneered the concept of training network systems engineers in the field

NEW MEDIA LITERACY

New media literacy is the ability to critically assess and develop content that uses new media forms and to leverage these media for persuasive communications.

ARCHIVE

{also use in Computational Thinking and Reliability}

(1)   annals; collection; documentation; files; place or keep records in archive; library store of data

Résumé bullet points:

• <u>Archived</u> large email and Internet data sources and multi-table joined information

AUDIO CONFERENCE

(1)   teleconference using only audio to communicate

Résumé bullet points:

• <u>Audio conferenced</u> AA/BS experience as Senior Producer for Fortune 500 accounts

AUTOMATE

(1)   computerize; mechanize; program

Résumé bullet points:

• <u>Automated</u> processes using SSIS or DTS for all business areas

BAR CODE

(1)   digital inventory; product codes

Résumé bullet points:

• <u>Bar coded</u> scanner IOS and Android for Web applications

BATCH PROCESS

{also use in Data Mind-Set}

(1)   process as a single unit or batch in automatic data processing

Résumé bullet points:

• <u>Batch processed</u> SQL scripting

CYBERNATE

{also use in Computer Literate}

(1) control a function, process, or creation by a computer

(1) The IT department <u>cybernated</u> nearly all office functions.

DATA MINE

{also use in Computational Thinking}

(1) retrieve facts and information from large databases
Résumé bullet points:

- <u>Date mined</u> for analysis online usage and customer interaction data using GM's preferred statistical package, SAS, and GM's preferred database software, Oracle SQL

DEBUG

{also use in Design Mind-Set}

(1) clear up; correct; eliminate errors or malfunctions; fix; mend; repair; restore; service; sort out
Résumé bullet points:

- <u>Debugged</u> department's software

DRILL DOWN

(1) go deeper for information; look for deeper or more subtle patterns or meaning; perform greater in-depth or subtle analysis of data
Résumé bullet points:

- <u>Drilled down</u> for more information and patterns to data

DROPBOX

{also use in Computer Literate}

(1) connect all of one's computers by software so that content such as photos, graphics, files, and so on are automatically transferred from one to another.

(1) Our remote sales team <u>dropboxed</u> the photos of its small group meetings.

E-BARTER

(1)   conduct bartering online, usually in a bartering exchange
Résumé bullet points:

• <u>E-bartered</u> for services and equipment not in budget

ENCODE

{also use in Creativity}

(1)   transform an idea into a set of symbols during communications process
Résumé bullet points:

• <u>Encoded</u> customer data in special-purpose binary format

ENCRYPT

(1)   encipher; encode

(2)   add an electronic digital code to software and data being sent over public
       network to prevent its unauthorized use
Résumé bullet points:

• <u>Encrypted</u> digital messages for maximum security

E-SOURCE

{also use in Computer Literate}

(1)   process and tools that electronically allow all activities in digital sourcing
       process
Résumé bullet points:

• <u>E-sourced</u> Six Sigma Promotions

E-TAIL

{also use in HARD SKILLS: Advertising and Business and Business Sense}

(1)   online retail selling and business activities
Résumé bullet points:

• <u>E-tailed</u> high-ticket luxury items

FACEBOOK

{also use in Communication and HARD SKILLS: Computer Literacy}

(1)   connect with someone online on the social network Facebook

(1) Many of our employees in other offices <u>Facebooked</u> each other to
hold their own virtual meeting.

HOT DESK

(1)   allow employees who work outside the office a lot to use any open desk
       when they come in to the office
Résumé bullet points:
   • Hot desked 100-person office, significantly reducing overhead

HYPERLINK

(1)   connect or join by a hyperlink to other online sites

*(1) Our Web page is hyperlinked to the pages of many of our vendors in
our value chain.*

MICRO PUBLISH

(1)   publish in greatly reduced form, especially on microfilm or microfiche
Résumé bullet points:
   • Micro published the hundreds of versions of field manuals

NETWORK

{also use in Professional Demeanor and Presence and Team Player, and
HARD SKILLS: Business and Business Sense}

(1)   complex; exchange ideas; interact with others to exchange information
       and develop contacts; make contacts; meet people; set up; use system of
       contacts
(2)   connect computer hardware in a system designed to support something
Résumé bullet points:
   • Networked with a diverse group of contacts

WEBCAST

(1)   send content for mass distribution by Internet

(1) The firm's annual meeting was Webcasted.

NOVEL AND ADAPTIVE THINKING

Novel and adaptive thinking is the proficiency at thinking and coming up with solutions and responses beyond that which is routine or rule based.

ACCLIMATE

{also use in Cognitive Load Management, Common Sense, Cross-Cultural Competency, Flexibility, Leadership, Learn, Professional Demeanor, Team Player, and Work Ethic}

(1) acknowledge or declare approval; applaud; cheer; hail; praise vociferously; sing one's praises

ACCOMPLISH

{also use in Accomplishments and Achievements, Accountability, Accuracy and Precision, Attention to Detail, Drive, Leadership, Motivated, Passion and Tenacity, and Work Ethic}

(1) achieve; attain; bring about; carry out; cause to happen; complete; do; gain; get done; finish; fulfill; make happen; make possible; produce; pull off; reach; realize; undertake

Résumé bullet point:

• Accomplished shift from shift operator to supervisor

ACHIEVE

{also use in Accomplishments and Achievements, Attitude, Drive and Passion, Education, Leadership, Motivated, Novel and Adaptive Thinking, Risk Tolerant, and Self-Confidence}

(1) accomplish; attain; complete; conclude; do; finish; get; perform; pull off; reach; realize

(2) succeed in doing something

Résumé bullet points:

• Achieved professional-level certification for Cisco Service Provider

ACTIVATE

{also use in Accomplishments and Achievements, Commitment and Dedication, Critical Thinking, and Problem Solving}

(1) acetify; become active; energize; galvanize; get going; initiate; make active; start; set in motion; set off; stimulate; trigger; turn off

(2)   call out militia or military for active duty

Résumé bullet points:

   • <u>Activated</u> backup systems during weather emergencies

ACTUALIZE

{also use in Accomplishments and Achievements, Attention to Detail, Common Sense, and Motivated}

(1)   make real or actual; realize

(2)   to fulfill the potential of
Résumé bullet points:

   • <u>Actualized</u> the career dreams of interns

AMELIORATE

{also use in Accomplishments and Achievements, Accountability, Accuracy and Preciseness, Attention to Detail, Creativity, Leadership, Learn, and Self-Manageable}

(1)   correct a mistake; improve; make better; tolerate

(2)   correct a deficiency or defect; make right a wrong; take action that makes up for one's negative or improper actions

CHAMPION

{also use in Accountability, Commitment and Dedication, Leadership, and Self-Confidence}

(1)   advocate; back; be a winner; campaign for; crusade for; excel; fight for; stand up for; support; uphold

   (1) Sharon <u>championed</u> the new commission plan for the sales team.

Résumé bullet points:

   • <u>Championed</u> development of software simulation and modeling methods to assist marketing in determining customer's "voice"—procedure is now standard operating procedure

FINDING AND FIXING PROBLEMS

(1)   identify problems and propose and implement effective solutions

INCENTIVIZE

(1)   encourage; provide one with a reason to work harder; provide with an incentive

Résumé bullet points:

* <u>Incentivized</u> customer service staff

OBVIATE

(1)   anticipate to prevent difficulties or disadvantages; avert; hinder; preclude; prevent

Outgoing, Friendly, and Positive Attitude

ACCEDE

{also use in Accountability, Commitment and Dedication, Customer Awareness, Flexibility, and Self-Manageable}

(1)   agree; allow; approach; ascend; attain; come to; comply; conform; consent; enter upon; give assent; grant; succeed to; take over

ACCOMMODATE

{also use in Accomplishments and Achievements, Compassionate, Cross-Cultural Competency, Customer Awareness, and Flexibility}

(1)   house; lodge; provide accommodations; put up

(2)   adapt; be big enough for; contain; have capacity for; hold; reconcile; seat

(3)   do a favor or a service for someone

(4)   adjust; become accustomed; familiarize; get used to; make suitable

(5)   allow for; assist; be of service; consider; find ways to help; oblige
<u>Collocates to: change, demand, desire, difference, growth, guest, need, request, passengers, schedule, space, special case(s), student</u>

ACKNOWLEDGE

{also use in Accountability, Honesty and Integrity, Learn, Professional Demeanor, and Self-Manageable}

(1)   admit; allow; avow; concede; confess; fess up; grant; own up; recognize

(2)   answer; react; reply; respond; return

(3)   greet; nod to; salute; wave to
Résumé bullet points:

* <u>Acknowledged</u> by industry association as one of the field's Top 50 Thought Leaders

ALLY

{also use in Cross-Cultural Competency and Social Intelligence}

(1)   align; associate; befriend; confederate; friend; helper; join; league; support

AMUSE

(1)   absorb; beguile; distract; divert; engross; entertain; interest; keep amused or busy; occupy; recreate

(2)   charm; divert; make laugh or smile; please

ASSOCIATE

(1)   ally; bind; combine; join; unite

(2)   friend

BUDDY UP

(1)   become overly friendly or familiar with someone

(2)   join with another person to do things together

CONCILIATE

{also use in Learn and Politeness}

(1)   appease; gain regard or goodwill by good acts; pacify; reconcile; soothe the anger of; win over

   (1) They <u>conciliated</u> rather than sought a settlement.

EMPATHIZE

{also use in Social Intelligence}

(1)   have compassion; identify with; sympathize; understand

(2)   undergo or feel empathy

EXALT

(1)   aggrandize; demand; dignify; elevate; ennoble; extort; glorify; impose; magnify; raise high in esteem; raise in dignity, status or honor; uplift

(2)   heighten the intensity of action or effect of

FRATERNIZE

(1)   associate; associate with in a brotherly manner; be on friendly terms; have intimate relations; keep company with

LAUD

{also use in Accountability, Communications, and Team Player}

(1)   to acclaim; applaud; celebrate; extol; mention; praise; speak well of

NURTURE

{also use in Compassionate}

(1)   cherish; provide extra care and attention in hopes of developing someone or something into full potential

    (1) I <u>nurtured</u> my networking contacts.

REACH OUT

(1)   extend support, help, or a favor to someone in need

    (1) Our group <u>reached out</u> to them as soon as we knew about their concerns.

POLITE, WELL MANNERED, COURTEOUS PHONE AND EMAIL ETIQUETTE

ACCORD

{also use in Social Intelligence}

(1)   bring about harmony and concurrence; cause to conform or agree; make an agreement

(2) bestow on someone
Résumé bullet points:

    • <u>Accorded</u> each the respect earned and deserved

AGREE

{also use in Accountability and Flexibility}

(1)   accord; affirm; concur; consent; get together; grant; harmonize; jibe; match; say yes; square

    (1) Tim <u>agreed</u> to apologize for the insult.

APPEAL

(1)   ask; call for; demand; petition for; request; urge

(2)   attract; charm; draw; fascinate; grab; interest; please; pull; tempt
Résumé bullet points:

    • <u>Appealed</u> to people's self-interest and needs

APPLAUD

(1)   admire; celebrate; clap; congratulate; express approval; praise; support
Résumé bullet points:

   • Applauded those who were deserving

ATONE

(1)   harmonize; expiate; reconcile

   (1) We all agreed that she had atoned with her good deeds.

COMPLY

(1)   abide; act in accordance; conform; follow; fulfill; meet the terms of;
       obey; observe; submit

   (1) I complied with the rule and paid the fine.

CONCILIATE

{also use in Learn and Outgoing}

(1)   appease; gain regard or goodwill by good acts; pacify; reconcile; soothe
       the anger of; win over

   (1) They conciliated rather than sought a settlement.

ENCOURAGE

(1)   abet; advance; promote; push; support

(2)   embolden; give courage, hope, and confidence to; hearten

(3)   be favorable to; foster; give support to; help
Résumé bullet points:

   • Encouraged and praised staff who put forth the effort

EXPIATE

(1)   apologize; atone; make amends; make up; pay the penalty for; redress;
       suffer

   *(1) The association expiated for the failure to use the donations properly
   by doubling the amount to the charity the next year.*

HELP

{also use in Accomplishments and Achievements and Compassionate}

(1)   abet; aid; assist; benefit; change for the better; improve; succor
Résumé bullet points:

- Helped new employees adjust to the corporate culture

LAVISH

(1)   give in great abundance; opulent; shower gifts; squander

(1) He lavished expensive gifts on his top sales people.

OBVIATE

(1)   anticipate to prevent difficulties or disadvantages; avert; hinder; preclude; prevent

PERMIT

(1)   allow; authorize; consent; give blessing to; grant permission to do something; okay; sanction

SHARE

{also use in Team Player}

(1)   communicate something; give one's portion to another; have in common; use jointly or in common

SMILE

(1)   have a favorable, agreeing, pleasurable appearance

(2)   regard with favor or approval

(3)   look with a favorable expression

SMOOTH OVER

(1)   fix a misunderstanding; reunite former friends who had been estranged; settle an argument; undo something that caused bad feelings

WELCOME

(1)   greet with pleasure and hospitality

YIELD

(1)   give way to another

(2)   produce or bear

(3)   give up to another; submit; surrender

(4)   give way to physical force

(5)   willingly give up a right, possession, or privilege

PROFESSIONAL DEMEANOR AND PRESENCE

ABIDE

{also use in Accountability, Commitment and Dedication, Common Sense, Cross-Cultural Competency, Reliability, Self-Manageable, and Work Ethic}

(1)   bear; continue; endure; go on being; put up with; stomach; take; tolerate

(2)   hold; remain; stand fast; stand for; stay

(3)   remain with someone

Collocates to: agreements, conditions, laws, norms, rules; resolutions, wishes

ABY

{also use in Reliability}

(1)   make amends for; pay the penalty for

ACCLIMATE

{also use in Cognitive Load Management, Common Sense, Cross-Cultural Competency, Flexibility, Leadership, Learn, Professional Demeanor, Team Player, and Work Ethic}

(1)   acclimatize; adapt; accustom yourself; adjust; become accustomed to a new environment or situation; familiarize; get used to

ACKNOWLEDGE

{also use in Accountability, Honesty and Integrity, Learn, Outgoing, and Self-Manageable}

(1)   admit; allow; avow; concede; confess; fess up; grant; own up; recognize

(2)   answer; react; reply; respond; return

(3)   greet; nod to; salute; wave to

Résumé bullet points:

- Acknowledged by industry association as one of the field's Top 50 Thought Leaders

ARTICULATE

{also use in Communication}

(1)   be eloquent; be fluent; express; communicate; convey; be lucid; put into words; state; tell; verbalize

BENCHMARK

{also use in Attention to Detail, Design Mind-Set, Learn; and HARD SKILLS: Advertising, Branding, PR, Sales, and Marketing; and HARD SKILLS: Business and Business Sense}

(1)   commence; identify and learn from the best business practices; leveled point of reference; standard; target

BOOST

(1)   advance; amplify; augment; enhance; further; heighten; hoist; improve; increase; lift; make better; raise

CEREBRATE

(ser´ ə brāt´)

{also use in Intelligence and Learn}

(1)   consider; ponder; think; use one's power of mind
Résumé bullet points:

  • Cerebrated with industry thought leaders and top management on strategic issues

CONSULT WITH CLIENTS

(1)   meet and learn client needs; understand client's business, operations, policies, and procedures
(2)   propose options to solve problems, issues, needs gap; propose solutions to client problems
Résumé bullet points:

  • Consulted with clients

CREDENTIAL

(1)   make official; receive or furnish with professional credentials

MANEUVER

(1)   carefully manipulate to achieve an end; specific tactic; finagle; jockey; manipulate; navigate; pilot; steer

MODERATE

(1)   curb; control; diminish; less extreme or intense; play down; regulate; restrain; temper; tone down

(2)   arbitrate; mediate; preside over; referee

NETWORK

{also use in New Media Literacy, Team Player, and HARD SKILLS: Business and Business Sense}

(1)   complex; exchange ideas; interact with others to exchange information and develop contacts; make contacts; meet people; set up; use system of contacts

RECOMMEND

(1)   advise as a course of action; advocate; counsel; make appealing or desirable; oppose; put forward with approval as being suitable; propose; suggest; urge

(2)   commend; endorse; mention; put in a good word; vouch for

REPRESENT

(1)   portray one's self in a particular way; signify; symbolize; or embody

SHOULDER

{also use in Accountability}

(1)   assume the burden or responsibility of

SPEARHEAD

{also use in Achievements and Accomplishments and Risk Tolerant}

(1)   be in front of something; lead; point; take the lead
Résumé bullet points:

   • Spearheaded the growth of global catalog business from $200,000 to $1,250,000 annually

TRANSCEND

(1)   carry on; conduct; exceed; excel; go beyond; perform; outdo; rise above; surpass

RELIABILITY, DEPENDABILITY, FOLLOW-THROUGH, AND RESPONSIBILITY

ABIDE

{also use in Accountability, Commitment and Dedication, Common Sense, Cross-Cultural Competency, Professional Demeanor, Self-Manageable, and Work Ethic}

(1)   bear; continue; endure; go on being; put up with; stomach; take; tolerate

(2)   hold; remain; stay; stand fast; stand for

(3)   remain with someone; to stay

Collocates to: agreements, conditions, laws, norms, rules; resolutions, wishes

ABOUND IN

(1)   be well supplied or have plenty of something in particular that is necessary or desired

ABY

{also use in Professional Demeanor}

(1)   make amends for; pay the penalty for

ACCEPT

{also use in Accountability, Cross-Cultural Competency, Take Direction, and Team Player}

(1)   agree; admit; believe; consent; say you will

(2)   receive with gladness and approval

(3)   receive; take something being offered

(4)   bow to; endure; put up with; resign yourself to; tolerate

ACCREDIT

{also use in Accountability, Attention to Detail, Customer Awareness, and HARD SKILLS: Administration and Organizational}

(1)   approve; attribute; authorize; credit to; endorse; recognize; sanction

(2)   certify; supply with credentials or authority

ADMINISTER

{also use in Accountability, HARD SKILLS: Auditing and Finance, Administrative Organizational, Planning and Time Management Self-Manageable}

(1)   control; deal out; direct; dispense; furnish a benefit; give out; govern; hand out; manage; mete out; order; run; supervise; oversee a process

ADVOCATE

{also use in Communications, Compassion, and Self-Manageable}

(1) advance; back; be in favor of; bolster; defend; encourage; promote; sponsor; support

ARCHIVE

{also use in Computational Thinking and New Media Literature}

(1)   annals; collection; documentation; files; place or keep records in archive; library; store of data

AUTHORIZE

(1)   accredit; commission; empower; enable; entitle; license; grant; qualify

CARRY THROUGH

{also use in Motivated, Team Player, and Work Ethic}

(1)   persist; put into action; take the most difficult

CERTIFY

{also use in Attention to Detail, Design Mind-Set, and Honesty and Integrity}

(1)   assure; attest; confirm; testify; verify; vouch; witness

DEPEND

(1)   bank on; count on; expect; influenced by; reckon; rely; trust in

ESTABLISH

{also use in Accomplishments and Achievements and Accountability}

(1)   begin; create; enact; ensconce; found; install; institute; prove; set up; settle; start
(2)   make firm; make stable
(3)   bring about; cause to happen

(4)   settle in an office or position

(5)   cause to be accepted or recognized; set up permanently

(6)   demonstrate; prove

EXPATIATE

{also use in Communications}

(1)   cover a wide scope of topics; elaborate

(2)   add details to an account or an idea

(3)   roam or wander freely

(4)   speak or write in great detail

FOLLOW THROUGH

{also use in Critical Thinking}

(1)   continue an action or activity; finish something you have started

FULFILL

{also use in Accomplishments and Achievements and Accountability}

(1)   carry out; complete an assignment; discharge; execute; exercise; implement; perform; satisfy

GIVE CREDENCE

(1)   consider an idea, concept, or plan as trustworthy or credible

INCULCATE

{also use in Social Intelligence}

(1)   impress a belief or idea on someone by repeating it over and over again until the idea is accepted

(2)   teach by persistent urging

(3)   implant ideas through constant admonishing

INSURE

(1)   assure; cover; guard; guarantee; indemnify; insist; promise; underwrite

JUSTIFY

(1)   account for; back; confirm; defend; excuse; explain; rationalize; prove or
       show to be right; maintain; vindicate
Résumé bullet points:

   • <u>Justified</u>, sourced, and supervised the installation of $24 million CAD
     assembly process

LEAD

(1)   be first; captain; command; conduct; control; direct the operations, activ-
       ity, or performance; head; escort; go ahead; go in front; guide on a way
       especially by going in advance; manage; officer; pilot; show the way
Résumé bullet points:

   • <u>Led</u> implementation of efficient purchasing and JIT inventory manage-
     ment system

MAINTAIN

{also use in HARD SKILLS: Administrative and Organizational}

(1)   cause or enable something to continue; keep something in good condi-
       tion; keep up; provide with the necessities for life and existence; support;
       sustain
Résumé bullet points:

   • <u>Maintained</u> perfect record for attendance and punctuality over nine years

PERFECT

(1)   bring to completion; make perfect or nearly perfect according to stan-
       dards; mistake free; without flaws
Résumé bullet points:

   • <u>Perfected</u> prototype design that reduced production time by 20%

PERSEVERATE

{also use in Attention to Detail and Design Mind-Set}

(1)   continue something; repeat something insistently or over and over again

PERSEVERE

{also use in Commitment and Dedication}

(1)   be steadfast in purpose; continue in some effort or course of action in
       spite of difficulty or opposition; persist

PERSIST

(1) endure; prevail; refuse to give up or quit; remain; take and maintain a stand

SATIATE

(1) gratify completely; glut with an excess of something; provide with more than enough; satisfy an appetite fully

TACKLE

(1) encounter; engage; face; take on; take hold of

(2) fasten by means of tackle

(3) harness a horse

(4) deal with a difficult person or situation

(5) knock or throw to the ground

TARGET

(1) aim; focus; reduce effort or cost to achieve objective

(2) establish as a target or goal

RISK TOLERANCE

ACHIEVE

{also use in Accomplishments and Achievements, Attitude, Drive and Passion, Leadership, Motivated, Novel and Adaptive Thinking, and Self-Confidence}

(1) accomplish; acquire; actualize; attain; complete; conclude; discharge; dispatch; do; earn; effect; enact; finish; get; manage; obtain; perform; pull off; reach; reach a goal; realize

(2) succeed in doing something

Résumé bullet points:

   • Achieved successful conclusion to longest union strike in firm's history

ACQUIRE

{also use in Accomplishments, Customer Awareness, Design Mind-Set, and Gather Data and Convert into Information}

(1)   attain; buy; come to possess; earn; gain; get; hold; obtain; purchase; receive

Résumé bullet points:

• Acquired the skills to work with latest technology

ACT

{also use in Leadership and Self-Manageable}

(1)   accomplish; acquit yourself; be active; behave; do something; operate; proceed; react; respond; take action; take steps; work

Résumé bullet points:

• Acted as facilitator for work group charged with migrating database to cloud

ACTUATE

{also use in Accomplishments and Achievements, Attention to Detail and Accuracy, Creativity, Customer Awareness, Leadership}

(1)   activate; arouse to action; motivate; put into motion; start; trigger

Résumé bullet points:

• Actuated work rules that improved productivity by 20 percent

ADUMBRATE

(1)   foreshadow; give a general description of something but not the details; obscure; overshadow; predict; prefigure; presage; summarize

ANTICIPATE

(1)   await; be hopeful for; expect; discussion or treatment; foresee and deal with in advance; give advance thought; look forward to; wait for; think likely

BETA TEST

{also use in Design Mind-Set, Leadership, and HARD SKILLS: Analytical, Research, Computational}

(1)   field test; sample prior to rollout; road test

BREAK THROUGH

{also use in Drive, Passion, Tenacity, and Risk Tolerant}

(1)   unexpected gain or improvement

(2)   develop a new idea or concept

BRANCH OUT

{also use in Cross-Cultural Competency}

(1)   add new interests or new activities; begin doing new things

CHALLENGE

(1)   contest; deft; dare

(2)   goal; obstacle; ordeal

CIRCUMVENT

{also use in Creativity}

(1)   avoid; dodge; evade; elude; frustrate by surrounding or going around; get
      around; go around; outwit; skirt; take another route; thwart

CRUSADE

{also use in Motivated and Self-Confident}

(1)   campaign for which one has placed a high priority; cause; drive; risk or
      stakes

DEFY

(1)   challenge; confront; dare; disobey; disregard; dissent; face front; flout;
      hurl defiance; mutiny; out dare; rebel; resist; revolt; rise up; stand up to

EXPERIMENT

{also use in HARD SKILLS: Analytical, Research, and Computational}

(1)   research; test; trial

(2)   make or conduct an experiment

(3)   try something new

GAMBLE

(1)   bet; hazard; risk; speculate; stake; venture; wager

KINDLE

(1)   arouse; fire; light; provoke; stir to action

SPEARHEAD

{also use in Achievements and Accomplishments and Professional Demeanor}

(1)   be in front of something; lead; point; take the lead
Résumé bullet points:

• <u>Spearheaded</u> three year relaunch and rebranding of legacy product

SELF-CONFIDENCE

ABREACT

{also use in Accountability and Communications}

(1)   release repressed emotions by acting out the situation in words, behavior, or imagination

ACCLAIM

{also use in Accomplishments and Achievements and Social Intelligence}

(1)   acknowledge or declare approval; applaud; cheer; hail; praise vociferously; sing one's praises

ACHIEVE

{also use in Accomplishments and Achievements, Attitude, Drive and Passion, Education, Leadership, Motivated, Novel and Adaptive Thinking, Risk Tolerant}

(1)   accomplish; attain; complete; conclude; do; finish; get; reach; perform; pull off; realize

(2)   succeed in doing something
Résumé bullet points:

• <u>Achieved</u> highest industry certification

ADVOCATE

{also use in Commitment and Dedication, Compassionate and Caring, and Reliability}

(1)   advance; back; be in favor of; bolster; defend; encourage; promote; sponsor; support

ANSWER FOR

(1) assume or take responsibility for

ATTRIBUTE

(1) accredit; ascribe; assign; attach; classify; connect; credit to; designate;
     impute; lay at someone's door; make part of

BLOVIATE

(1) hold forth in a pompous self-centered way; orate verbosely; speak
     pompously and at length

BOAST

(1) brag; cause for pride; crow; display; enjoy; feature; pride yourself in;
     show off; swank

BOUNCE BACK

(1) rebound; recover from misfortune or mishap

BRING AROUND

(1) convince someone to accept a new prostitution or opinion; persuade

CARRY THE WATER

{also use in Commitment and Dedication, Customer Awareness, Leadership,
and Work Ethic}

(1) bear the main responsibility for something

CHAMPION

{also use in Accountability, Commitment and Dedication, Leadership, and
Novel and Adaptive Thinking}

(1) advocate; back; be a winner; campaign for; crusade for; excel; fight for;
     stand up for; support; uphold

CHERRY-PICK

(1) choose the best thing; choose something carefully; elect; opt; single out

CONTRAST

(1) compare; counter; counterpoint; create a gap; differ; distinguish; diverge;
     draw a distinction; have a disparity; set off; stand out against

CRUSADE

{also use in Motivated and Risk Tolerant}

(1)   campaign for which one has placed a high priority; cause; drive; risk or stakes

DISPLAY

(1)   bear; brandish; disport; exhibit; expose; flash; flaunt; make apparent; make visible; parade; present; reveal; show; show off

EMULATE

{also use in take direction}

(1)   copy; follow; imitate; work or strive to copy something admired

(2)   try often by copying or imitating a model

(3)   rival successfully

ESTABLISH

{also use in Accomplishments and Achievements, Accountability, and Reliability}

(1)   begin; create; enact; ensconce; found; install; institute; prove; set up; settle; start

(2)   make firm; make stable

(3)   bring about; cause to happen

(4)   settle in an office or position

(5)   cause to be accepted or recognized; set up permanently

(6)   demonstrate; prove

GIN UP

{also use in Accomplish and Common Sense}

(1)   create; encourage; increase; produce

INNERVE

{also use in Communication and Social Intelligence}

(1)   call to action; provoke; stimulate something

PINPOINT

(1)   find or locate exactly; identify; isolate; pin down

PIONEER

{also use in Accomplishments and Achievements, Creativity, Drive, Passion and Tenacity, Self-Confidence, and Self-Manageable}

(1)   be the first to develop new ideas or concepts; lead the way

QUARTERBACK

(1)   direct; get the plan started; lead; manage; plan; strategize; take charge

REACH BACK

(1)   extend one's self to exert extra effort to achieve a goal or objective

(2)   think or remember something from long past in attempt to connect to current issue or point

RESCUE

(1)   bring back from failure or near failure; free, resuscitate; save or secure from danger or failure

RISK

(1)   chance; exposure to danger, failure or hazard for the potential reward

SHOOT THE MOON

(1)   work a high-risk strategy where you gain everything and your opponent loses everything

SHOWCASE

(1)   display results of one's work; exhibit to good advantage

SELF-MANAGEABLE, WORK INDEPENDENTLY

ABIDE

{also use in Accountability, Commitment and Dedication, Common Sense, Cross-Cultural Competency, Professional Demeanor, and Work Ethic}

(1)   bear; continue; endure; go on being; put up with; stomach; take; tolerate

(2)   hold; remain; stand fast; stand for; stay

(3)   to remain with someone

Collocates to: agreements, conditions, laws, norms, rules; resolutions, wishes

ABSORB

{also use in Accomplishments and Achievements, Cognitive Load Management, Commitment and Detail, Common Sense, Cross-Cultural Competency, Flexibility, and Learn}

(1)   assimilate; acquire; attract; consume; digest; endure; engulf; fascinate; imbibe; soak up; sustain; take in; use up

(2)   draw into oneself; grasp; realize; recognize; take in; understand

(3)   become captivated, engaged or preoccupied in; fascinated; interested
Résumé bullet points:

- Absorbed the work of departments that have been eliminated, doubling my responsibilities

ACCELERATE

{also use in Accomplishments and Achievements, Commitment and Dedication, HARD SKILLS: Time and Organizational Management, and Motivated}

(1)   gather speed; go faster; grow; hurry; increase speed of; pick up the pace; quicken; rush; speed up

(2)   cause to occur sooner

ACCRUE

{also use in Critical Thinking and Problem Solving}

(1)   accumulate; amass; build up; ensue; increase; mount up

(2)   come to one as a gain; amass

(3)   accrete; add; grow by addition

ACKNOWLEDGE

{also use in Accountability, Honesty and Integrity, Learn, Outgoing, and Personal Demeanor}

(1)   admit; allow; avow; concede; confess; fess up; grant; own up; recognize

(2)   answer; react; reply; respond; return

(3)   greet; nod to; salute; wave to
Résumé bullet points:

- Acknowledged by industry association as one of the field's Top 50 Thought Leaders

ACT

{also use in Leadership and Risk Tolerant}

(1) accomplish; acquit yourself; be active; behave; do something; take action; take steps; operate; proceed; react; respond; work

(2) act out; appear in; feign; impersonate; mock; perform; play in; pretend; simulate

ADDRESS

{also use in Attention to Detail and Communications}

(1) direct one's attention to; discourse; lecture; remark; speak directly to; talk to

(2) deliver; direct; dispatch; forward; mark with a destination; refer

(3) adopt; attend to; concentrate on; deal with; focus on; take up

ADMINISTER

{also use in Accountability, Reliability, HARD SKILLS: Accounting and Finance, and Administrative, Organizational, Planning and Time Management}

(1) control; deal out; direct; dispense; furnish a benefit; give out; govern; hand out; manage; mete out; order; run; supervise; oversee a process

Résumé bullet points:

- Administered and proctored online certification exams for national career development training

ADVANCE

{also use in Accomplishments and Achievements}

(1) continue; evolve; forward; further; go ahead; go forward; increase; move ahead; move forward; move on; press forward; press on; proceed; progress

(2) build up; develop; enhance; expand; promote; rise; spread

ADVOCATE

{also use in Communications, Compassion, and Reliable}

(1) advance; back; be in favor of; bolster; defend; encourage; promote; sponsor; support

ALERT

(1) intelligent; look out for; make aware of impending trouble or danger; watch

ALIGN

{also use in Attention to Detail, Commitment and Dedication, Design Mind-Set, and Social Intelligence}

(1)   ally; adjust; bring oneself into agreement with; correct; level; parallel; straighten

(2)   arrange something in reference to something else

AMASS

{also use in Accomplishments and Achievements, Drive and Passion, Education, and Self-Manageable}

(1)   accrue; accumulate; assemble; build up; collect; compile; gather together; hoard; pile up; store up

Résumé bullet points:

  • Amassed 75 customer appreciation letters and recommendations

AMELIORATE

{also use in Accomplishments and Achievements, Accountability, Accuracy and Preciseness, Attention to Detail, Creativity, Leadership, Learn, Novel and Adaptive Thinking}

(1)   correct a mistake; improve; make better; tolerate

(2)   correct a deficiency or defect; make right a wrong; take action that makes up for one's negative or improper actions

ANSWER FOR

(1)   assume or take responsibility for

APPLY

(1)   affect; be appropriate; be valid; concern; correlate; exercise; pertain; relate

(2)   ask for; put in; request

(3)   direct; employ; harness; operate; put into operation; use; utilize

(4)   put on; rub on; smear; spread over

(5)   attach to; fix to; join; stick to

APPOINT

(1)   assign; delegate; design; designate; determine; employ; make; take on

APPROVE

{also use in Accountability and Design Mind-Set}

(1) accept; agree to; attest; back up; command; commend; endorse; favor; praise; ratify; sanction; support

(2) allow; authorize; consent; grant; pass; sanction

ASSIST

{also use in Cognitive Load Management, Compassionate, and Team Player}

(1) abet; collaborate; facilitate; help with

AVERT

(1) avoid; divert; forestall; miss; prevent; stop happening; turn away; ward off

BARGAIN

(1) agree; barter; contract; covenant; deal; haggle; negotiate between parties; make a pact; reach accord; make a transaction; reach an understanding

BOOTSTRAP

{also use in Common Sense and Design Mind-Set}

(1) initiative; manage without assistance; succeed with few resources

BREAK THROUGH

{also use in Drive, Passion, Tenacity, and Risk Tolerant}

(1) unexpected gain or improvement

(2) new idea

BULL DOG

(1) attack something viciously and ferociously; overcome a difficult obstacle or challenge

CALL THE SHOTS

(1) direct the outcome of an activity or affair; predict the outcome of something

CAPTAIN

(1) be in command; lead; command; control; manage something; skipper

COLLABORATE

{also use in Accomplishments and Achievements, Communication, Cross-Cultural Competency, Take Direction, and Work Ethic}

(1)   act as a team; assist; cooperate; pool resources; team up; work jointly with; work together

Résumé bullet points:

- Collaborated with training and education providers to ensure courses offered were beneficial to workers

COMPILE

{also use in Computational Thinking and Data Gathering}

(1)   collect and edit something; gather and put together in an orderly form

COMPLETE

{also use in Accomplishments and Achievements, Accountability, Commitment and Dedication, Education, and Work Ethic}

(1)   choate; conclude; be done; entire; finish a task intact; integral; perfect; through; unabridged; uncut; whole; wrap up

Résumé bullet points:

- Completed all major job responsibilities without the need for constant direct supervision, thus helping the manager reallocate her time to be more productive

CONCEIVE

{also use in Accomplishment and Achievements, Accountability, and Critical Thinking and Problem Solving}

(1)   create; envisage; imagine; invent original idea; picture; visualize

(2)   begin life; dream; elaborate; form; make up

CONTROL

{also use in Accomplishments and Achievements, and HARD SKILLS: Administrative and Organizational}

(1)   be in charge of; be in command; direct; dominate; govern; have influence or power over; manage; organize; oversee; rule; run

COORDINATE

{also use in Accomplishments and Achievements, Attention to Detail, Critical Thinking, Problem Solving, and HARD SKILLS: Administrative and Organizational}

(1)   bring together; combine; direct; harmonize; manage; match up; organize; synchronize; work together

COPE

(1)   deal with; encounter; get by; hack it; fight or content with; handle; manage; match; meet; muddle through; survive

CULTIVATE

{also use in Commitment and Dedication, Customer Awareness, Intelligence, and Social Intelligence}

(1)   develop; encourage; foster; help; nurture; promote; refine; support

(2)   tend to; till; work on

DEFUSE

(1)   calm; cool; harmless; make less harmful or dangerous; harmless; make less tense; mollify; neutralize; placate; rescue; resolve; save; smooth out; soothe

DEVELOP

(1)   achieve; advance; build up; evolve; expand; exploit; expound; extend; generate; gain; grow; increase; mature; strengthen; unfold; widen

(2)   make known gradually
Résumé bullet points:

  • Developed first multimedia in-house sales operation with one person to cover two state territories previously covered by three outside sales reps; increased sales by 25 percent, increased retention of customers by 15 percent, and lowered costs by 50 percent

DISENTANGLE

{also use in Cognitive Thinking and Design Mind-Set}

(1)   clear; free from entanglements and ties; find solutions to problems; straighten out

DIG INTO

(1)   begin the process of something; begin to examine something thoroughly; go to work on something

(2)   delve; poke around; research; understand

ENGENDER

(1)   bring about or into being; cause; create; give rise to; originate; produce

ENGROSS

(1)   absorb; busy; involve; hold

(2)   take the entire attention of; occupy wholly

(3)   express formally or in legal form

ESPOUSE

(1)   adopt; advocate; back; champion; promote; support; take up

FIRM UP

(1)   arrange; put details together

HANDLE

{also use in Accountability and HARD SKILLS: Administrative and Organizational}

(1)   carry out; come to grips with; conduct; control; cope with; deal with; have overall influence; manage; manipulate; ply; process; run; see to; sort out; supervise; take responsibility for; undertake; wield

(2)   feel; finger; hold; manage with the hands; touch
Résumé bullet points:

   • Handled more than $4,000 per day in cash sales

IMPROVISE

(1)   ad-lib; extemporize; fake; make; invent or arrange offhand; fabricate out of what is conveniently on hand; spur of the moment

INITIATE

{also use in Accomplishments and Achievements, and Critical Thinking}

(1) begin; create; commence; inaugurate; induct; install; instate; instigate; introduce; invest; kick off; open; set off; start

(2) coach; instruct; mentor; teach; train; tutor

MASTERMIND

(1) control, direct, engineer, supervise, or otherwise be the brains behind

PIONEER

{also use in Accomplishments and Achievements, Creativity, Drive, Passion and Tenacity, Motivated, and Self-Confidence}

(1) be first to develop new ideas or concepts; lead the way

PREPARE

(1) arrange; get ready to deal with something; make ready for use or consideration; organize; plan; practice; put in order

(2) coach; groom; make ready; train; warm up

REBUT

(1) argue in opposition; confute; contradict; deny; disprove; invalidate; oppose; refute

(2) show to be false

RESTORE

(1) rebuild to original state; replace; replenish

(2) give back; make restitution

(3) put back in place, position, or rank

(4) bring back to health or strength

SAVE

(1) keep from danger; rescue; save from danger, harm, or evil

(2) preserve; put up; store for future use

(3) avoid need to use or spend

(4) prevent or guard against loss, waste, or misuse

SEGUE

{also use in Cognitive Load Management and Time Management}

(1) continue without break; lead into new areas; proceed without interruption; smooth change to next topic

SOLO

(1) act independently; perform alone

(2) fly alone

TAKE RESPONSIBILITY FOR

(1) personally accept the outcome of something

SOCIAL INTELLIGENCE

Social intelligence is the ability to connect with others in a deep and direct way—to sense and stimulate reactions and desired interactions.

ABET

{also use in Accountability, Commitment and Dedication, Learn, and Motivated}

(1) advocate; assist; back; back up; encourage; espouse; foment; help incite; put up to; sanction; support; urge (especially in wrongdoing)

ACCEDE

{also use in Accountability, Commitment and Dedication, Customer Awareness, Flexibility, Outgoing, and Self-Manageable}

(1) agree; allow; approach; ascend; attain; come to; comply; conform; consent; enter upon; give assent; grant; succeed to; take over

ACCLAIM

{also use in Accomplishments and Achievements and Self-Confident}

(1) acknowledge or declare approval; applaud; cheer; hail; praise vociferously; sing one's praises

ACCORD

{also use in Polite}

(1) bring about harmony and concurrence; cause to conform or agree; make an agreement

(2) bestow on someone

ACQUAINT

{also use in Cross-Cultural Competency}

(1) accustom; aware; explain; familiar with; inform; introduce; know; notify; present; run by; tell

(2) come to know personally

ACQUIESCE

{also use in Accountability, Attitude, Cognitive Load Management, and Compassion}

(1) accept; agree; assent; comply with passively; concede; concur; consent; give in; go along with; submit; yield

ADMIRE

(1) adulate; appreciate; approve; enjoy; esteem; have a positive feeling toward one; like; marvel; regard; relish; think highly of

AGGREGATE

{also use in Computational Thinking and HARD SKILLS: Administrative and Organizational}

(1) accumulate; amass; collect; combine; gather together; sum; total; whole

ALIGN

{also use in Attention to Detail, Commitment and Dedication, Design Mind-Set, and Self-Manageable}

(1) ally; adjust; bring oneself into agreement with; correct; level; parallel; straighten

(2) arrange something in reference with something else

ALLY

{also use in Cross-Cultural Competency and Outgoing}

(1) align; associate; befriend; confederate; help; league; join; support

BAND TOGETHER

(1) bar; combine; disallow; forbid; gang; group; unite in opposition to something; interdict; outlaw; proscribe; veto

BUDDY UP

{also use in Outgoing}

(1) become overly friendly or familiar with someone

(2) join with another person to do things together

CEDE

(1)   abandon; abdicate; admit; assign; concede; give or hand over; give up; grant; let go; relinquish; render; surrender; transfer; yield

CLOSE RANKS

{also use in Compassionate}

(1)   stand together; unite; work together

COALESCE

{also use in Accomplishments and Achievements, Accountability, Commitment and Dedication, Cognitive Load Management, Cross-Cultural Competency, Flexibility, Learn, and Team Player}

(1)   combine; come together as one; grow together; join; unite

COHERE

{also use in Compassionate and Team Player}

(1)   bond; go together; hold fast; join together

CONFIDE

(1)   breathe; disclose; divulge; entrust; make known; pass on; reveal; share; tell; whisper
(2)   entrust; deposit with; give to; place with

CONNECT

(1)   associate; attach; combine; fasten; interrelate; join; relate; unite

CONSULATE

(1)   comfort; give hope in time of grief
(2)   empathize; sympathize

CONTRIBUTE

{also use in Drive, Passion, Tenacity, and Work Ethic}

(1)   chip in; come across; come through; donate; give or supply in common with; kick in; subscribe

COOPERATE

{also use in Commitment and Dedication}

(1)   act together; agree; associate; co-adjudge; collaborate; social capital; work together for a common purpose

COUNSEL

{also use in Attitude, Communication, and Compassionate}

(1)   advise; deliberate; guide; inform; mentor

COUNTENANCE

{also use in Compassion}

(1)   approve; encourage; favorably dispose; sanction; support

CRITIQUE

(1)   analyze and evaluate; critically review

CULTIVATE

{also use in Commitment and Dedication, Customer Awareness, Intelligence, and Self-Manageable}

(1)   develop; encourage; foster; help; nurture; promote; refine; support

EDIFY

{also use in Cognitive Load Management, Communications, Compassionate, Intelligence, and Learn}

(1)   educate; enlighten; illuminate; improve; inform; instruct; teach

(2)   uplift morally, spiritually, or intellectually

ELUCIDATE

{also use in Accountability, Cognitive Load Management, Communication, Take Direction, and HARD SKILLS: Analytical, Research, and Computational}

(1)   clarify; explain; explicate; expose; expound; illuminate; lucid; make something clear; reveal; throw light on it

EMPATHIZE

{also use in Outgoing}

(1)   have compassion; identify with; sympathize; understand

(2)   undergo or feel empathy

ENTICE

(1)   allure; beguile; lure; persuade; tempt

(2)   attract by offering hope, reward, or pleasure

(3)   cajole or lure someone

ENTRUST

(1)   place something or someone into the protection of someone

(2)   charge or invest with a trust or duty

(3)   assign the care of; turn over for safekeeping

EXCITE

(1)   arouse; call forth; inspire; provoke; put into action; stir to action

GALVANIZE

{also use in Critical Thinking and Leadership}

(1)   activate; propel someone or something into sudden action; stimulate

GIVE VOICE

(1)   tell what you or your interest group thinks and feels

IMMERSE

(1)   absorb; bury; dip; engross; throw yourself into

(2)   occupy the full attention of

INCULCATE

{also use in Reliability}

(1)   impress a belief or idea on someone by repeating it over and over again
      until the idea is accepted

(2)   teach by persistent urging

INDIVIDUALIZE

(1) adapt to the needs or special circumstances of an individual; distinguish; particularize

INGRATIATE

(1) curry favor; gain favor or favorable acceptance for by deliberate effort; defer to; make acceptable to another

INNERVE

{also use in Communication and Self-Confidence}

(1) call to action; provoke; stimulate something

INSORB

{also use in Learn}

(1) absorb; incorporate; take in

INSPIRE

{also use in Creativity}

(1) affect; arouse; encourage; excite; impel; incite; prompt; provoke; motivate; stimulate; stir

INTERMESH

(1) come or bring together; engage; intermesh; interweave; merge ideas and concepts

INVIGORATE

(1) animate; energize; enliven; galvanize; increase; liven; refresh; revitalize; strengthen; stimulate

TAKE DIRECTION, FOLLOW DIRECTIONS, WILLING TO TAKE DIRECTIONS

ACCEDE

(1) agree; allow; approach; ascend; attain; come to; comply; conform; consent; enter upon; give assent; grant; succeed to; take over

ACCEPT

{also use in Accountability, Cross-Cultural Competency, Reliability, and Team Player}

(1)   admit; agree; believe; consent; say you will

(2)   receive with gladness and approval

(3)   receive; take something being offered

(4)   bow to; endure; put up with; resign yourself to; tolerate

ADJURE

{also use in Communication}

(1)   beg; change under oath; renounce under oath; request earnestly

ANSWER

{also use in Communication}

(1)   come back with; counter; react; reply; respond; rejoin; retort

(2)   explain one's actions or behavior

COLLABORATE

{also use in Accomplishments and Achievements, Commitment and Dedication, Communication, Cross-Cultural Competency, Self-Manageable, and Work Ethic}

(1)   act as a team; assist; cooperate; pool resources; team up; work jointly with; work together

Résumé bullet points:

   • Collaborated closely with project management teams and relevant stakeholders to ensure necessary resources were made available

DUPLICATE

(1)   copy; double; make twice as good; mirror

EDIT

{also use in Accountability, Attention to Detail, and Communication}

(1)   alter; correct; revise and make ready

(2)   prepare a written work for publication by selection, arrangement, and annotation

(3)   make additions, deletions, or other changes

ELUCIDATE

{also use in Accountability, Cognitive Load Management, Communication, HARD SKILLS: Analytical, Research, and Computational, and Social Intelligence}

(1) clarify; explain; explicate; expose; expound; illuminate; lucid; make something clear; reveal; throw light on it

EMULATE

{also use in Self-Confidence}

(1) copy; follow; imitate; work or strive to copy something admired

(2) try often by copying or imitating a model

(3) rival successfully

ENGAGE

(1) bind by a promise; engross; involve; occupy; participate; pledge; tie up

(2) arrange for the services of; employ; hire

(3) arrange for the use of; reserve

(4) draw into; involve

(5) attract and hold; employ and keep busy; occupy

(6) mesh together

Résumé bullet points:

- Engaged with the strategic business plan as it relates to the overall mission and goals established by the board

FINE-TUNE

(1) make fine adjustments; regulate

IMPUTE

(1) accredit; ascribe a result or quality to anything or anyone; assign; attribute; fix

(2) accuse; allege; assert; challenge; charge; cite; implicate

LEARN

(1) gain knowledge from experience, observation, or being taught

MAKE GOOD

(1) do what was promised; make something come true

MANUFACTURE

{also use in Engineering and R&D}

(1)   assemble; build; construct; create; develop; make; produce

MONITOR

(1)   keep under observation; watch so as to regulate; control or record

OBSERVE

{also use in Design Mind-Set, Gather Data and Convert into Information, and HARD SKILLS: Analytical, Research, and Computational}

(1)   examine; make a remark; monitor; notice; perceive; say; scrutinize; study; survey; view; watch attentively

UNDERSTOOD

(1)   perceive the intended meanings of something

(2)   interpret or view in a particular way

(3)   infer from information received

(4)   assume that something is present or is the case

TEAM PLAYER, TRANSDISCIPLINARY SKILLS, WORKS WELL WITH OTHERS ACROSS DEPARTMENTS AND DISCIPLINES, AND AS A MEMBER OF VIRTUAL TEAMS

ACCEPT

{also use in Accountability, Cross-Cultural Competency, Reliability, and Take Direction}

(1)   admit; agree; believe; consent; consider; hold as truth; say you will

(2)   receive with gladness and approval

(3)   receive; take something being offered

(4)   bow to; endure; put up with; resign yourself to; tolerate
Collocates to: challenge, fact, gift, idea, invitation, offer, position, role, responsibility

ACCLIMATE

{also use in Accountability, Cognitive Load Management, Cross-Cultural Competency, Flexibility, Leadership, Learn, Novel and Adaptive Thinking, Professional Demeanor, and Work Ethic}

(1) acclimatize; accustom yourself; adapt; adjust; become accustomed to a new environment or situation; familiarize; get used to

ASSENT

{also use in Compassionate}

(1) accede; accept; acquiesce; agree; concur; consent

ASSIST

{also use in Cognitive Load Management, Compassionate, and Self-Manageable}

(1) abet; collaborate; facilitate; help with

CARRY THROUGH

{also use in Motivated, Reliability, and Work Ethic}

(1) persist; put into action; take the most difficult

COADJUTE

{also use in Cross-Cultural Competency}

(1) cooperate; work together

COALESCE

{also use in Accomplishments and Achievements, Accountability, Cognitive Load Management, Commitment and Dedication, Cross-Cultural Competency, Flexibility, Leadership, Learn, Social Intelligence}

(1) combine; come together as one; grow together; join; unite

COHERE

{also use in Compassion and Social Intelligence}

(1) bond; go together; hold fast; join together

COLLATE

{also use in Accomplishments and Achievements, Cogitative Load Management, Design Mind-Set, and HARD SKILLS: Gather Data and Convert to Information}

(1) assemble or collect to compare; bring together; gather; pool; pull together

INCREASE

{also use in Accountability}

(1) add to; amplify; augment; boost; enhance; enlarge; improve; multiply; raise; swell

(2) encourage; foster; fuel; intensify; redouble; strengthen

(3) escalate; expand; grow; multiply; mushroom; proliferate; rise; soar; spread; swell

Résumé points:

- Increased customer retention by 50 percent over two years, helping to improve profits

- Increased operating performance by 20 percent while reducing labor coast by $500,000

- Increased profit margins and revenues through product mix diversification and targeted marketing

JOIN

(1) agree with the agenda, beliefs, and view of something and be willing to follow certain standards signifying one's acceptance

(2) agree to conditions; become a member associate; combine; enlist; enroll; enter; muster in; sign on

LAUD

{also use in Accountability, Communications, and Outgoing}

(1) acclaim; applaud; celebrate; extol; mention; praise; speak well of

NETWORK

{also use in Professional Demeanor and Presence and New Media Literacy}

(1) complex; exchange ideas; interact with others to exchange information and develop contacts; make contacts; meet people; set up; use system of contacts

SERVE

{also use in Compassionate}

(1) aid; assist; be of use; do services for; help; perform duties; treat in a certain way

SHARE

{also use in Polite}

(1) communicate something; give one's portion to another; have in common; use jointly or in common

TEAM BUILD

{also use in Leadership}

(1) create cooperative group dynamics

TIME MANAGEMENT

ACCELERATE

{also use in Accomplishments and Achievements, Commitment and Dedication, Motivated, Self-Management, and HARD SKILLS: Time and Organizational Management}

(1) gather speed; go faster; grow; hurry; increase speed of; pick up the pace; quicken; rush; speed up

(2) cause to occur sooner

CONSERVE

(1) avoid waste; husband; keep from being damaged; preserve; save

DELIBERATE

{also use in Critical Thinking}

(1) confer; consider; consult; debate; meditate; mull over; plan; ponder; reflect; think carefully; weigh carefully

DELIMIT

{also use in Attention to Detail, Critical Thinking and Problem Solving, and Design Mind-Set}

(1) define; demarcate; determine; fix boundaries; restrict; set limits; state clearly

DIVE INTO

(1) start immediately on something

EARMARK

{also use in Accountability, Accuracy and Preciseness, Attention to Detail, and Commitment and Dedication}

(1) allocate; allot; appropriate; assign; set aside or reserve for special purpose

ENGINEER

{also use in Critical Thinking and HARD SKILLS: Engineering}

(1)   cause; coax; make happen

(2)   plan, construct and manage as an engineer

(3)   guide; plan and direct skillfully; superintend

EXPEDIT

{also use in Drive and Passion and Time Management}

(1)   accelerate; hurry up; rush

(2)   speed up or make easy the process of or action of

(3)   dispatch; issue officially; send off

HIE

(hī)

{also use in Design Mind-Set}

(1)   hurry or hasten; move very fast

MULTITASK

(1)   work on several tasks at the same time

PACE

(1)   move or develop (something) at a particular rate or speed

PLAN

{also use in Problem Solving and HARD SKILLS: Time, Organizational, Planning and Time Management}

(1)   arrange; design; have in mind a project or purpose; intend; prepare; purpose; set up

(2)   arrange strategic ideas in diagrams, charts, sketches, graphs, tables, maps, and other documents

Résumé bullet points:

- <u>Planned,</u> coordinated, and supervised all aspects of database center relocation from the West Coast to Atlanta, Georgia, with no impact on service

QUICKEN

(1)   animate; enliven; revive

(2)   arouse; stimulate; stir

(3)   cause to move more rapidly; hasten

SCHEDULE

{also use in Attention to Detail}

(1)   make arrangements or a plan for carrying out something

(2)   plan events and activities for certain times

SEGUE

{also use in Cognitive Load Management and Self-Manageable}

(1)   continue without break; lead into new areas; proceed without interruption; smooth change to next topic

ZOOM THROUGH

(1)   get through something quickly

WORK ETHIC

ABIDE

{also use in Accountability, Commitment and Dedication, Common Sense, Cross-Cultural Competency, Professional Demeanor and Presence, Reliability, and Self-Manageable}

(1)   bear; continue; endure; go on being; put up with; stomach; take; tolerate

(2)   hold; remain; stand fast; stand for; stay

Collocates to: agreements, conditions, laws, norms, rules, resolutions, wishes

ACCLIMATE

{also use in Cognitive Load Management, Common Sense, Cross-Cultural Competency, Flexibility, Leadership, Learn, Novel and Adaptive Thinking, Professional Demeanor, and Team Player}

(1)   acclimatize; accustom yourself; adapt; adjust; become accustomed to a new environment or situation; familiarize; get used to

ACCOMPLISH

{also use in Accomplishments and Achievements, Accountability, Accuracy and Precision, Attention to Detail, Drive, Passion and Tenacity, Leadership, Motivated, and Novel and Adaptive Thinking}

(1)   achieve; attain; bring about; carry out; cause to happen; complete; do; gain; get done; finish; fulfill; make happen; make possible; produce; pull off; reach; realize; undertake

ADJUST

{also use in Accountability, Common Sense, Cross-Cultural Competency, Engineering, Flexibility, and R&D}

(1)   accommodate; alter; amend; attune; bend; change; correct; fine-tune; fix; modify; pacify; rectify; regulate; resolve; settle; tune up; tweak

BACKSTOP

{also use in Commitment and Dedication and Common Sense}

(1)   act as a backstop; use as a measure of last resort in case of an emergency

BUOY UP

(1)   carry; elate; encourage; hold up; lift

CANVAS

(1)   campaign; count; debate; drum up support; electioneer; solicit

(2)   ballot; investigate; poll; research; seek; survey; test

CARRY THE WATER

{also use in Commitment and Dedication, Customer Awareness, Leadership, and Self-Confidence}

(1)   bear the main responsibility for something

CARRY THROUGH

{also use in Motivated, Reliability, and Team Player}

(1)   persist; put into action; take the most difficult

COLLABORATE

{also use in Accomplishments and Achievements, Commitment and Dedication, Communication, Cross-Cultural Competency, Self-Manageable, and Take Direction}

(1)   act as a team; assist; cooperate; pool resources; team up; work jointly with; work together

COMPLETE

{also use in Accomplishments and Achievements, Accountability, Commitment and Dedication, Education, and Self-Manageable}

(1) be done; choate; conclude; entire; finish a task intact; integral; perfect; through; unabridged; uncut; whole; wrap up

Résumé bullet points:

- • <u>Completed</u> all job and extracurricular organizational civic requirements with highest proficiency ratings among 100 employees for five straight years

CONTRIBUTE

{also use in Drive, Passion, Tenacity, and Social Intelligence}

(1) chip in; come across; come through; donate; give or supply in common with; kick in; subscribe

DOUBLE DOWN

(1) doubling one's effort; significantly increasing the risk of one's involvement

DIG DEEP DOWN

(1) do more; put maximum effort into some endeavor; try extra hard

(2) donate as much as possible for a good cause

EMPOWER

{also use in Accountability and Drive, Passion, and Tenacity}

(1) allow; authorize; give authority or power to; sanction

(2) make one stronger and more confident, especially in controlling his life and claiming his rights

EXCEL

{also use in Drive, Passion, and Tenacity}

(1) shine; stand out; surpass

(2) be better, greater, or superior to others in the same field, profession, or endeavor

EXERT

(1) apply; exercise; use

(2) put forth or use energetically; put into action

(3) apply with great energy or effort

FAST TRACK

{also use in Drive, Passion, and Tenacity and HARD SKILLS: Business and Business Sense}

(1)   bypass others; move a job ahead on a faster pace than normal; rapidly accomplish; speed up process

Résumé bullet points:

  • <u>Fast tracked</u> database projects

HELD DOWN THE FORT

(1)   be willing to take on tough jobs; take on tougher assignments alone; work without much assistance

HUNKER DOWN

{also use in Commitment and Dedication}

(1)   become determined not to budge from an opinion or position; circle the wagons; get in defensive position; prepare for bad news or prolonged assault; prepare for siege

MEASURE UP

(1)   be equal; of full high quality

OPTIMIZE

{also use in HARD SKILLS: Accounting and Finance}

(1)   make the best or most effective use of a situation or resource

OVERACHIEVE

{also use in Motivated}

(1)   do or perform better than expected

PARTICIPATE

(1)   chip in; contribute; involve oneself; join in; partake; share in; take part

CHAPTER 3

Hard Skills

ACCOUNTING AND FINANCE

ADJUST

{also use in Accountability, Common Sense, Cross-Cultural Competency, Flexibility, and Work Ethic}

(1)   accommodate; alter; amend; attune; bend; change; correct; fine-tune; fix; modify; pacify; rectify; regulate; resolve; settle; tune up; tweak

Résumé bullet points:

- <u>Adjusted</u> to Sage accounting software

ADMINISTER

{also use in Accountability, HARD SKILLS: Administrative, Organizational, Planning and Time Management, Reliability, and Self-Manageable}

(1)   control; deal out; direct; dispense; furnish a benefit; give out; govern; hand out; manage; mete out; order; oversee a process; run; supervise

Résumé bullet points:

- <u>Administered</u> accounts payable system

AUDIT

{also use in Attention to Detail, Computational Thinking, and Design Mind-Set}

(1)   appraise; assess; check; count; examine; inspect; review; verify the accounting records of

Résumé bullet points:

- <u>Audited</u> corporate client reports containing equities, fixed income, and derivatives

BALANCE

(1) assess; calculate; collate; compare; consider; evaluate; even out; equalize; keep upright; offset; settle; square; stabilize; stay poised; steady; tally; total; weigh; weight up

Résumé bullet points:

  • Balanced all books and completed state and federal tax forms

CALCULATE

{also use in Accountability, Computational Thinking, Engineering, and R&D}

(1) account; coax; compute; consider; deem; determine something; entice; enumerate; figure; persuade; rate

Résumé bullet points:

  • Calculated P/E ratios, DCF, EPS, NPV, and beta for equity security analysis

COLLECT

(1) accumulate; amass; assemble; bring together; gather; pull together

(2) have a passion for; hoard; save; stockpile

Résumé bullet points:

  • Collected 90 percent of 180-day past due accounts

COMPUTE

{also use in Critical Thinking, HARD SKILLS: Computational Thinking, and Software Developing}

(1) calculate; determine a number; equate; figure

Résumé bullet points:

  • Computed midcap investment options using free float market capitalization weighted method

MAXIMIZE

{also use in Accomplishments and Achievements, SOFT SKILLS: Accountability, and Drive, Passion and Tenacity}

(1) make best use of; make as great or as large as possible; raise to the highest possible degree

Résumé bullet points:

  • Maximized limited advertising budget by using coop ads and sponsors

OPTIMIZE

{also use in SOFT SKILLS: Work Ethic}

(1)   make the best or most effective use of a situation or resource

PROJECT

{also use in SOFT SKILLS: Design Mind-Set}

(1)   estimate; expect; forecast; plan; propose; scheme

(2)   extend outward toward something else

Résumé bullet points:

* <u>Projected</u> five-year cash flow

QUANTIFY

{also use in Attention to Detail, Critical Thinking and Problem Solving, and HARD SKILLS: Analytical, Research, and Computational}

(1)   express something in quantifiable terms

(2)   express or explain something numerically

(3)   determine, express, or explain the quantity of, numerical measure of, or extent of

RATIOCINATE

{also use in SOFT SKILLS: Attitude and Design Mind-Set}

(1)   work toward a solution through logical thinking and reason

REALLOCATE

(1)   distribute; newly allocate; opportune; set apart

RECALCULATE

(1)   calculate again; refigure

RECAPITALIZE

(1)   convert debt into stock or shares

RECTIFY

{also use in Accountability and HARD SKILLS: Accounting and Finance}

(1)   amend; correct; fix; put right; resolve; set right

(2)   adjust; cure; mend; remedy; repair

(3)   convert

REFINANCE

(1)   new capital or funds for a project

REMIT

(1)   pay what is due

(2)   abate; cancel; decrease; diminish; forgive or pardon; lessen; reduce

(3)   cancel

(4)   dispatch; forward; pay; send

(5)   pass on; refer; submit

REMUNERATE

(1)   settle debt or other financial obligations

(2)   pay or compensate for work done

RESTRUCTURE

{also use in HARD SKILLS: Business and Business Sense}

(1)   downsize; reorganize; resize

(2)   plan or provide for new structure

(3)   change the terms of a loan to reduce the burden on the debtor

SOLVE

{also use in Accomplishments, Creativity, and Design Mind-Set}

(1)   find a solution; settle

(2)   provide or find a suitable answer to a problem

TABULATE

{also use in Attention to Detail, Computational Thinking, and HARD SKILLS: Analytical, Research, and Computational}

(1)   add up; chart; count; put facts in a table or column tally; total

ADMINISTRATIVE, ORGANIZATIONAL, TIME, AND PLANNING SKILLS

ACCELERATE

{also use in Accomplishments and Achievements, Commitment and Dedication, Motivated, Self-Manageable, and HARD SKILLS: Time and Organizational Management}

(1) gather speed; go faster; grow; hurry; increase speed of; pick up the pace; quicken; rush; speed up

(2) cause to occur sooner

ACCREDIT

{also use in Accountability, Attention to Detail, Customer Awareness, and Reliable}

(1) approve; attribute; authorize; credit to; endorse; recognize; sanction

(2) certify; supply with credentials or authority

ACT ON

{also use in Attention to Detail and HARD SKILLS: Time and Organizational Management}

(1) specific course of action; respond to

ACTIVATE

{also use in Commitment and Dedication, Critical Thinking, and Problem Solving}

(1) acetify; become active; energize; galvanize; get going; initiate; make active; set in motion; set off; start; stimulate; trigger; turn off

ADMINISTER

{also use in Accountability, Reliability, HARD SKILLS: Accounting and Finance, and Self-Manageable}

(1) control; deal out; direct; dispense; furnish a benefit; give out; govern; hand out; manage; mete out; order; oversee a process run; supervise
Résumé bullet points:

  • <u>Administered</u> National Windows NT 4.0/Exchange Server 4.0 with 3,000 users

AGGREGATE

{also use in Computational Thinking and Social Intelligence}

(1) accumulate; amass; collect; combine; gather together; sum; total; whole

ARRANGE

{also use in Accountability and Creativity}

(1) array; authorize; catalogue; classify; fix; order; organize; position; set up

(2) make plans for something to be done

ASSIGN

{also use in Accountability, Accuracy and Preciseness, and Computational Thinking}

(1)   allocate; allot; choose; consign; dispense; dole out; give; hand over; pick; select; transfer

(2)   appoint; delegate; designate; detail; name

CACHE

(1)   accumulate; collect; hide; hoard; store; supply

CENTRALIZE

{also use in Attention to Detail and Design Mind-Set}

(1)   bring power of something to the central organization; consolidate

CHOREOGRAPH

(1)   arrange; compose; direct

COLLOCATE

(1)   arrange; catalog; set up

CONTROL

{also use in Accomplishments and Achievements and Self-Manageable}

(1)   be in charge of; be in command; direct; dominate; govern; have influence or power over; manage; organize; oversee; rule; run

COORDINATE

{also use in Accomplishments and Achievements, Attention to Detail, Critical Thinking, and Problem Solving}

(1)   bring together; combine; direct; harmonize; manage; match up; organize; synchronize; work together

Résumé bullet points:

  • Coordinated with industry compliance consultants and product managers to verify applications and meet regulatory compliance

DELIBERATE

{also use in Critical Thinking and Time Management}

(1)   confer; consider; consult; debate; meditate; mull over; plan; ponder; reflect; think carefully; weigh carefully

DOCUMENT

(1)   detail; give proof; record; verify; write down

FACILITATE

(1)   aid; assist; ease; help

FINESSE

(1)   be adroit; outmaneuver; skillfully handle

FOSTER

(1)   advance; encourage; promote; support

HANDLE

{also use in Accountability and Self-Manageable}

(1)   carry out; come to grips with; conduct; control; cope with; deal with; have overall influence; manage; manipulate; ply; process; run; see to; sort out; supervise; take responsibility for; undertake; wield

 (2)   feel; finger; hold; manage with the hands; touch

Résumé bullet points:

• <u>Handled</u> online reservations and answered reference inquires

IMPLEMENT

{also use in Accomplishments and Achievements and Accountability}

(1)   accomplish; apply; carry out; complete; effect; employ; enforce; execute; finish; fulfill; instigate; put into action; put into operation; put into place; put into practice; put into service; realize; use

MAINTAIN

{also use in Reliable}

(1)   cause or enable something to continue; keep something in good condition; keep up; provide with the necessities for life and existence; support; sustain

Résumé bullet points:

• <u>Maintained</u> document sets and all revisions for four mid-range servers

MANAGE

{also use in Accomplishments and Achievements and HARD SKILLS: Business and Business Sense}

(1)   administer; be in charge of; conduct or direct affairs; oversee; regulate; run; supervise

(2)   do; fare; fend; get along; get by; make do; muddle through

(3)   control the behavior of; handle; succeed in dealing with

(4)   succeed despite difficulties

Résumé bullet points:

- • <u>Managed</u> successful launch of branch location

OPERATE

(1)   be in effect; bring about a desired or appropriate effect; control the function of; have a certain influence

Résumé bullet points:

- • <u>Operated</u> crane, backhoes, conveyer belts, bends, and loaders in multi-faceted work

ORGANIZE

(1)   arrange systematically; categorize; make arrangements, plans, or preparations for; order; put in order; sort out; systematize

(2)   control; coordinate; fix; manage; take charge

Résumé bullet points:

- • <u>Organized</u> workforce for large hotel

OVERSAW

{also use in Accountability and HARD SKILLS: Business and Business Sense}

(1)   administer; control; direct; keep an eye on; manage; run; supervise

Résumé bullet points:

- • <u>Oversaw</u> sales force and house accounts fee calculation for slow-moving product, increasing sales by 50 percent in one year

PLAN

{also use in Critical Thinking and Problem Solving}

(1)   arrange; design; have in mind a project or purpose; intend; prepare; set up

(2)   arrange strategic ideas in diagrams, charts, sketches, graphs, tables, maps, and other documents

Résumé bullet points:

- <u>Planned</u> and implemented server moves to brand new data center in Utah, including specifications, implementation, and support for EMC Clarion SAN storage solution

ADVERTISING, BRANDING, PUBLIC RELATIONS, SALES, AND MARKETING (ALSO SEE BRANDING, MARKETING, SALES EXPERIENCE)

BENCHMARK

{also use in Attention to Detail, Design Mind-Set, HARD SKILLS: Business and Business Sense, Learn, and Professional Demeanor}

(1)   commence; identify and learn from the best business practices; level a point of reference; standard; target

Résumé bullet points:

- <u>Benchmarked</u> a number of industrial calls to close

BIRD DOG

(1)   follow; observe; watch for the purpose of learning

CLICK STREAM

(1)   count and observe consumer behavior on Web sites

Résumé bullet points:

- <u>Click streamed</u> Web site traffic for market growth, product optimization, increased profitability, and enhanced customer satisfaction

CO-BRAND

(1)   advertise, market, promote in conjunction with another brand

Résumé bullet points:

- <u>Co-branded</u> credit card with American Express

COLLABORATE

(1)   act as a team; assist; cooperate; pool resources; team up; work jointly with; work together

Résumé bullet points:

- <u>Collaborated</u> with other stakeholders to create a customer-centric value chain

CONDUCT NEEDS ANALYSIS

(1)   analyze gap between needs and delivered goods/services; audit, examine
Résumé bullet points:

> • <u>Conducted needs analysis</u> for new franchise territories

CROWD SOURCE

{also use in Common Sense}

(1)   identify a group with common demographic or psychographic character-
      istics and determine how to best make contact with them to deliver a mes-
      sage such as a sales or advertising message
Résumé bullet points:

> • <u>Crowd sourced</u> three start-up firms

DIRECT MARKET

(1)   use a database to target and market selected products, services, or con-
      cepts to individuals with an identifiable need or desire through interactive
      multimedia marketing channels
Résumé bullet points:

> • <u>Direct marketed</u> previously low-margin products sold by sales force,
>   increasing overall profits for line by 23 percent

E-TAIL

{also use in New Media Literacy and HARD SKILLS: Business and Business
Sense}

(1)   sell retail and conduct business activities online

HYPERLINK/HOT LINK

(1)   connect by a hyperlink or hotlink; join a digital community, blog, Web
      site, or other social media
Résumé bullet points:

> • <u>Hyperlinked</u> Web site with partners and sponsors, increasing site traffic
>   by 40 percent

MARKET

(1)   advertise; offer to sell; promote
Résumé bullet points:

> • <u>Marketed</u> new products into new markets, achieving profitability in 18
>   months

MASS MARKET

(1) produce, market, and distribute a large volume of a single product, idea, concept, or service to one consumer marketplace

Résumé bullet points:

- • <u>Mass marketed</u> high-ticket aspirational goods, successfully employing saturation pricing

MERCHANDIZE

{also use in HARD SKILLS: Business and Business Sense}

(1) market goods; promote selling of goods

Résumé bullet points:

- • <u>Merchandised</u> electronics and communications equipment

STORYBOARD

(1) create; lay out; plan; strategize

(2) make a storyboard

Résumé bullet points:

- • <u>Storyboarded</u> creative troubleshooting problems

TEST MARKET

{also use in HARD SKILLS: Business and Business Sense}

(1) sample; try something in limited scope

Résumé bullet points:

- • <u>Test marketed</u> product appeal prior to launch

ANALYTICAL/RESEARCH, COMPUTATIONAL, AND MATH

ACCOUNT FOR

{also use in Attendance and Punctuality, Attention to Detail and HARD SKILLS: Business Sense}

(1) have available; have at hand; consider; analyze; explain

(2) know the state of or whereabouts of something or someone

ANALYZE

{also use in Attention to Detail, Critical Thinking, and HARD SKILLS: Gather Data and Convert into Information}

(1)   consider; dissect; evaluate; examine; explore; interpret; investigate; probe; question; scrutinize; study

Résumé bullet points:

- <u>Analyzed</u> quantitative data

ARRAY

{also use in Attention to Detail and Design Mind-Set}

(1)   gamut; place in an orderly arrangement; set out for display or use

(2)   marshal troops; parade; place an order

(3)   dress in fine or showy attire

Résumé bullet points:

- <u>Arrayed</u> data in JavaScript

ASSERT

{also use in Design Mind-Set}

(1)   affirm; allege; aver; avow; claim; contend; declare; emphasize; protest; state strongly; stress

(2)   champion; defend; establish; insist upon; maintain; make a claim for; stand up for; support; uphold

BETA TEST

{also use in Design Mind-Set, Leadership, and Risk Tolerant}

(1)   field test; road test; sample prior to rollout

Résumé bullet points:

- <u>Beta tested</u> cloud accounting software

CALCULATE

{also use in Accountability, Accounting and Finance, Computational Thinking, and Accounting and Finance}

(1)   account; coax; compute; consider; deem; determine something; entice; enumerate; figure; persuade

Résumé bullet points:

- <u>Calculated</u> statistical significance and confidence of polls

CIPHER

(1)   ascertain by mathematics; calculate

COMPUTE

{also use in Critical Thinking, Accounting and Finance, and Software Developing}

(1)   calculate; determine a number; equate; figure; make a mathematical calculation

(1) I computed the cost of the new material in just minutes.

Résumé bullet points:

• Computed tomography angiograms

CONVEY

{also use in Communication}

(1)   conduct; express; lead; make known; pass; put into words

(2)   bring; carry; move; take from one place to another; transfer

CORRELATE

{also use in Attention to Detail, Computational Thinking, and Cross-Cultural Competency}

(1)   associate; bring into mutual relation; calculate or show the reciprocal relation between; come together; correspond; parallel

Résumé bullet points:

• Correlated subquery (also known as a synchronized subquery)

DELINEATE

{also use in Accountability, Attention to Detail, and Communication}

(1)   describe accurately; determine; draw an outline; identify or indicate by marking with precision; fix boundaries; represent something

ELUCIDATE

{also use in Accountability, Cognitive Load Management, Communication, Social Intelligence, and Take Direction}

(1)   be lucid; clarify; explain; explicate; expound; expose; illuminate; make something clear; reveal; throw light on it

EXPERIMENT

{also use in Risk Tolerant}

(1)   research; test; trial

(2)   make or conduct an experiment

(3)   try something new

EXTRAPOLATE

{also use in Cogitative Load Management and Critical Thinking}

(1)   construct an image; estimate; infer

(2)   arrive at conclusion or results by hypothesizing from known facts or observations

HYPOTHESIZE

{also use in Cogitative Load Management and Critical Thinking}

(1)   make educated guess of some outcome

(2)   be lucid clarify; explain; make something clear; explicate; expose; expound; illuminate; reveal; throw light on it

OBSERVE

{also use in Design Mind-Set, Gather Data and Convert into Information, and Take Direction}

(1)   examine; make a remark; monitor; notice; perceive; say; scrutinize; study; survey; view; watch attentively

POSIT

{also use in Accountability, Attention to Detail, Critical Thinking and Problem Solving}

(1)   assume; conceive; conjecture; hypothesize; imagine; postulate; put forward; speculate; state or assume as fact; suggest; theorize

POSTULATE

{also use in Communication}

(1)   assume; claim; guess; hypothesize; look for a reason or take for granted without proof; propose; put forward; suggest

QUANTIFY

{also use in Attention to Detail, Critical Thinking, and HARD SKILLS: Accounting and Finance}

(1)   express something in quantifiable terms

(2)   express or explain numerically

(3) determine, express, or explain the quantity of, numerical measure of, or extent of

RESEARCH

(1) make an inquiry; survey; investigate thoroughly
Résumé bullet points:

- Researched, analyzed, and recommended new technology
- Researched proper components for clients, ensuring value, reliability, and substantial savings

RUMINATE

{also use in Communications and Critical Thinking}

(1) chew over; cogitate; contemplate; mull over; ponder; reflect on; think over

(2) mediate; turn over in one's mind

SIMULATE

(1) imitate; model; pretend

(2) use a computer simulation to represent

SURMISE

(1) assume; conclude; conjecture; construe; deduce; gather; guess; hypothesize; imagine; postulate; presume; speculate; suppose; suspect; theorize; work out

TABULATE

{also use in Attention to Detail, Computational Thinking, and HARD SKILLS: Accounting and Finance}

(1) add up; chart; count; put facts in a table or column; tally; total

BUSINESS AND BUSINESS SENSE

ACCOUNT FOR

{also use in Analytical, Research, and Computational, Attendance and Punctuality, Attention to Detail, and HARD SKILLS: Business Sense}

(1) analyze; consider; explain; have available; have at hand

(2) know the state of or whereabouts of something or someone

BANKROLL

(1)   finance; supply money for a project

(2)   privately fund a capital investment

Résumé bullet points:

    • <u>Bankrolled</u> two entrepreneurial start-ups

BENCHMARK

{also use in Attention to Detail, HARD SKILLS: Advertising, Branding, PR, Sales, and Marketing, HARD SKILLS: Business and Business Sense, Learn, and Professional Demeanor}

(1)   commence; identify and learn from the best business practices; level a
      point of reference; standard; target

Résumé bullet points:

    • <u>Benchmarked</u> the start-up costs for a small business

BRAND

(1)   identify differently; separate by some identity

CONSIGN

(1)   agree; dispatch; entrust; pack off; relegate; submit

(2)   deliver; send; transfer

CROWD FUND

(1)   raise money from multiple individuals online for a start-up business

DIVERSIFY

{also use in Cross-Cultural Competency and Flexibility}

(1)   branch out; expand; spread out; vary

DOWN SCOPE

(1)   downsize a project; reevaluate whether a project should be done

Résumé bullet points:

    • <u>Down scoped</u> low-volume business units

DOWNSCALE

(1)   cut back in size or scope; economize; rationalize; scale back; slim down;
      trim

DYNAMIC PRICE

(1)   rapidly move prices as a result of supply or demand matching

(1) We employed <u>dynamic pricing</u> to deal with the rapid increase in the fall in consumer demand.

E-TAIL

{also use in HARD SKILLS: Advertising and New Media Literacy}

(1)   conduct retail business activities online

FAST TRACK

{also use in Drive, Passion, Tenacity, and Work Ethic}

(1)   move someone or something in an accelerated manner, past normal requirements, time limitations, and experience

(2)   bypass others; move rapidly; speed up

Résumé bullet points:

   • <u>Fast tracked</u> database projects

FRANCHISE

(1)   control; own; trademark

GLOBALIZE

(1)   make worldwide in scope or application

HIRE

(1)   grant the personal service of someone; take or offer employment

KICK THE TIRES

(1)   be first to investigate; check for early warning signs; look into something by checking the obvious things

(1) As the economic conditions worsened, I <u>kicked the tires</u> of all new funding requests.

LICENSE

(1)   accredit; allow; authorize; certify; grant permit

Résumé bullet points:

   • <u>Licensed</u> the firm's products in 15 global markets

MANAGE

{also use in Accomplishments and Achievements, Administrative, Organization, and Planning}

(1)   administer; be in charge of; conduct or direct affairs; oversee; regulate; run; supervise

(2)   do; fare; fend; get along; get by; make do; muddle through

(3)   control the behavior of; handle; succeed in dealing with

(4)   succeed despite difficulties

Résumé bullet points:

  • <u>Managed</u> the in-house key accounts, accounting for 25 percent of total sales

MERCHANDIZE

{also use in Advertising, Branding, PR, Sales, Marketing}

(1)   market goods; promote selling of goods

MERGE

(1)   blend gradually into something else; combine two or more organizations into one; mix

(1) The second and third largest firms <u>merged</u> and became the industry leader.

NEARSHORE

(1)   move business operations such as manufacturing, customer service, and human resources back to the home country; reshore

Résumé bullet points:

  • <u>Nearshored</u> half of firm's previously international manufacturing operations, creating 4,000 US jobs

NETWORK

{also use in Professional Demeanor and Presence and Team Player}

(1)   complex; exchange ideas; interact with others to exchange information and develop contacts; make contacts; meet people; set up; use system of contacts

(1) I <u>networked</u> my way into several great job interviews.

OVERSAW

{also use in Accountability and HARD SKILLS: Administrative and Organizational}

(1)   administer; control; direct; keep an eye on; manage; run; supervise
Résumé bullet points:

- <u>Oversaw</u> the merger and acquisition that accounted for tripling the size of the firm in four years

PROMOTE

(1)   help bring about the growth or popularity of something or someone
Résumé bullet points:

- <u>Promoted</u> to section chief

PROTOTYPE

{also use in Creativity}

(1)   create models and replicas of what is to be produced

RECHANNEL

(1)   reassign resources or attention; redirect along a desired path
Résumé bullet points:

- <u>Rechanneled</u> $20 million of value channel partnership resources into developing just in time parts allocation system for new products

RESHORE

(1)   move business operations such as manufacturing, customer service, and human resources back to the home country; nearshore

RESTRUCTURE

{also use in HARD SKILLS: Accounting and Finance}

(1)   downsize; reorganize; resize

(2)   plan or provide for new structure

(3)   change the terms of a loan to reduce the burden on the debtor
Résumé bullet points:

- <u>Restructured</u> the firm's long-term debt, saving $33 million in interest payments

RETOOL

(1)   reengineer; rebuild; redesign

(2)   adapt; rethink the plan to meet new conditions
Résumé bullet points:

  • Retooled 170,000 square foot plant in less than 30 days, allowing pro-
    duction to resume before that of top competitors

ROLL OUT

(1)   start a campaign after a test; start a new product

(2)   begin a process from one point with ongoing plans to complete

(3)   flatten into sheets by rolling
Résumé bullet points:

  • Rolled out $35 million rebranding campaign to relaunch firm under new
    ownership

SET GOALS

(1)   create targets and objectives; make plans

STOVE PIPE

{also use in Design Mind-Set}

(1)   stack strategies, ideas, or plans
Résumé bullet points:

  • Stove piped marketing, communications, and financial ideas to have
    them ready to implement on short notice

SUPERVISE

(1)   administer; control; direct; handle; observe; organize; oversee; manage;
      run; take charge of; watch
Résumé bullet points:

  • Supervised, instructed, and scheduled nine staff members
  • Supervised six paralegal and secretarial staff

TEST MARKET

{also use in Advertising, Branding, PR, Selling, and Marketing}

(1)   sample; try something in limited scope
Résumé bullet points:

  • Test marketed beta test products

COMPUTER LITERATE

ANALYZE EVALUATION DATA

(1)   Interpret results from research, testing, or lab work
Résumé bullet points:

  • Analyzed evaluation data

COMPUTERIZE

(1)   operate or produce by means of a computer

(2)   equip with computers

CONVERT

(1)   change for equal value; change from one form to another; commute; lead; metamorphose; mutate; transfer; transfigure; transform; transmute; turn

CYBERNATE

{also use in New Media Literacy}

(1)   control a function, process, or creation by a computer

DROPBOX

{also use in New Media Literacy}

(1)   connect all of one's computers by software so that content such as photos, graphics, and files are automatically transferred from one to another

E-SOURCE

{also use in New Media Literacy}

(1)   process and tools that electronically allow all activities in digital sourcing process

FACEBOOK

{also use in Communications and New Media Literacy}

(1)   connect with someone online on the social network Facebook

GOOGLE

{also use in New Media Literacy}

(1)   check a reference on a Google site; search online for word or phrase

(2)   gaze; see; look intently

MASH UP

(1) combine songs or digital content into a new file

(2) brew or infuse

(3) combine two or more Web sites into a single site

STYLEFLEX

{also use in Communications}

(1) deliberate attempt to adjust one's communications style to accommodate others

(1) Too many people have <u>styleflexed</u> their communications styles.

ENGINEERING, RESEARCH, AND DEVELOPMENT, INCLUDING SOFTWARE, NEW PRODUCTS, AND SERVICES

ADAPT

{also use in Accomplishments and Achievements, Attention to Detail, Commitment and Dedication, Common Sense, Creativity, Cross-Cultural Competency, and Flexibility}

(1) acclimate; accommodate; adjust; change; conform; fashion; fit; get used to; make suitable; reconcile; square; suit; tailor

(2) make fit, often by modification

(3) cause something to change for the better

Résumé bullet points:

- <u>Adapted</u> unified communications solutions which increased organizational agility, saving businesses time and money

ANALYZE EVALUATION DATA

(1) interpret results from research, testing, or lab work

Résumé bullet points:

- <u>Analyzed evaluation data</u>

ASSEMBLE

(1) accumulate; combine; convene; group; mass produce; produce standardized goods in large volumes; unite

Résumé bullet points:

- <u>Assembled</u> PCBA prototyping process output

ASSESS EMPLOYEE AND CLIENT TRAINING NEEDS

(1)   analyze, audit, examine, and evaluate employee and client needs for training and education

Résumé bullet points:

- Assessed employee and client training needs and developed in-house training and development solution which accomplished all objectives and saved firm $250,000 annually

BUILT

{also use in Accountability and Customer Awareness}

(1)   construct; erect; put up; raise; rear

(2)   grow; improve; increase

Résumé bullet points:

- Built IE 6 computers from board level, installed operating systems and software, and configured systems

CALCULATE

{also use in Accountability, Accounting and Finance, and Computational Thinking}

(1)   account; coax; compute; consider; deem; determine something; entice; enumerate; figure; persuade

Résumé bullet points:

- Calculated P/E ratios, DCF, EPS, NPV, and beta for equity security analysis

CONDUCT NEEDS ANALYSIS

(1)   audit, examine, and analyze gap between needs and delivered goods/services

Résumé bullet points:

- Conducted needs analysis for major accounts

DESIGN

{also use in Accomplishments and Achievements, Creativity, and HARD SKILLS: Computer Literate, Engineering, and Research}

(1)   aim; contrive; devise; intend; make designs; mean; plan; propose; set apart for some purpose

(2) conceive; construct; create; draw up blueprints or plans; fabricate; invent; originate

(3) blueprint; cast; chart; contrive; draw up; frame; intent; map; project; set out

Résumé bullet points:

- <u>Designed</u> and implemented global Windows 2008 production/test environment for firm's six locations

DEVELOP AND DELIVER

{also use in Accomplishments and Achievements and Creativity}

(1) create, invent, put together, and produce output

(2) achieve; advance; build up; evolve; expand; exploit; expound; extend; gain; generate; grow; increase; mature; strengthen; unfold; widen

Résumé bullet points:

- <u>Developed and delivered</u> online engineering fluid flow simulator

ENGINEER

{also use in Critical Skills and Time Management}

(1) cause; coax; make happen

(2) plan, construct, and manage as an engineer

(3) guide; plan and direct skillfully; superintend

Résumé bullet points:

- <u>Engineered</u>, troubleshot, and fully documented IIS solutions

FIX

{also use in Accomplishments and Achievements and Critical Thinking}

(1) mend; replace; restore

Résumé bullet points:

- <u>Fixed</u> challenging electrical engineering problems to avoid the high risk and repercussions from downtime

IMPLEMENT SOLUTIONS

(1) accomplish; apply; carry out; complete; effect; employ; enforce; execute; finish; fulfill; instigate; put into action; put into operation; put into place; put into practice; put into service; realize; use

Résumé bullet points:

- <u>Implemented solutions</u> for corporate network architecture of 2,500 person firm with 6 locations

IMPROVE

{also use in Accomplishments and Achievements, Accountability, and HARD SKILLS: Research and R&D}

(1)   ameliorate; amend; better; build up; develop; employ; enhance in value; enrich; expand; further; get better; help; increase; make better; meliorate; perfect; raise to a better quality; upgrade use

Résumé bullet points:

* Improved operations that were adopted and made benchmarks by the industry trade association

INNOVATE

{also use in Creativity}

(1)   begin with something new; create; derive; devise; coin; commence; instigate; invent; make; modernize; originate; remodel; renew; renovate; transform; update; revolutionize

Résumé bullet points:

* Innovated solutions for unique problems with mechanical, electrical, and fluid systems

INSTALL

(1)   establish in an indicated place; position; put into use; set up for service or use

Résumé bullet points:

* Installed aggressive materials improvement and equipment refurbishing program

INVENT

(1)   concoct; contrive; cook up; create; devise; dream up; fabricate; formulate; hatch; imagine; make up; think up

Résumé bullet points:

* Invented core technologies

MAKE

{also use in Accomplishments and Achievements}

(1)   assemble; become; build; cause; compose; construct; create; develop; do; enact; erect; execute; fabricate; fashion; forge; form; frame; manufacture; mold; prepare; produce; put together; require; shape

Résumé bullet points:

- <u>Made</u> Industry "Top Ten Performers" five consecutive years (2007–2012)

MANAGE DEVELOPMENT

(1)   oversee, manage, and supervise process of creating or developing an asset
Résumé bullet points:

- <u>Managed development</u> of 3D prototyping

MANUFACTURE

{also use in Take Direction}

(1)   assemble; build; construct; create; develop; make; produce

(2)   concoct; fabricate; invent; make up
Résumé bullet points:

- <u>Manufactured</u> with six-axis robots

GATHER DATA AND CONVERT TO INFORMATION

ACQUIRE

{also use in Accomplishments, Customer Mind-Set, Design Mind-Set, and Risk Tolerant}

(1)   attain; buy; come to possess; earn; gain; get; hold; obtain; purchase; receive
Résumé bullet points:

- <u>Acquired</u> census tract data and merged it into customer database

ANALYZE

{also use in Attention to Detail, Critical Thinking, and HARD SKILLS: Analytical, Research, and Computational}

(1)   consider; dissect; evaluate; examine; explore; interpret; investigate; probe; question; scrutinize; study
Résumé bullet points:

- <u>Analyzed</u> customer data

CLASSIFY

{also use in Attention to Detail and Computational Thinking}

(1) arrange; assort; catalog; categorize; class; distribute into groups; grade; group; list by some order or sequence; organize; sort

Résumé bullet points:

- • Classified datasets

CODIFY

{also use in Computational Thinking}

(1) organize into a system of rules, codes, or principles to make clear and coherent

Résumé bullet points:

- • Codified data to prompt diagnosticians
- • Codified rating system to rank the industry's more efficient logistics systems

COLLATE

{also use in Accomplishments and Achievements, Cogitative Load Management, Design Mind-Set, and Team Player}

(1) assemble or collect to compare; bring together; gather; pool; pull together
Résumé bullet points:

- • Collated binary search or half-interval search algorithms

COLLECT

{also use in Leadership and Management and HARD SKILLS: Gather Data and Convert into Information}

(1) accumulate; amass; assemble; bring together; gather; pull together
Résumé bullet points:

- • Collected customer retention data

COMPILE

{also use in Computational Thinking and Self-Manageable}

(1) collect and edit something; gather and put together in an orderly form
Résumé bullet points:

- • Compiled data on cycle time for plant closings

DISCOVER

{also use in Accomplishments and Achievements, Common Sense, Critical Thinking and Problem Solving, and Intelligence}

(1)   ascertain; be first to learn something; determine; expose; find out; hear; learn; realize, see, or uncover something

Résumé bullet points:

   • <u>Discovered</u> the level of personal identifiable information consumers would be willing to give up in exchange for more personalized products

GATHER

(1)   accumulate; assemble; collect; come together; garner; group; harvest

Résumé bullet points:

   • <u>Gathered</u> detailed data on competitors

OBSERVE

{also use in Design Mind-Set, Gather Data and Convert into Information, Take Direction}

(1)   examine; make a remark; monitor; notice; perceive; say; scrutinize; study; survey; view; watch attentively

VERIFY

(1)   check; prove; validate

(2)   confirm or substantiate; prove to be true by demonstration, evidence, or testimony

(3)   check or confirm the accuracy of

Résumé bullet points:

   • <u>Verified</u> trades and hedges

Chapter 4

Experience, Credentials, Education

ACCOMPLISHMENTS AND ACHIEVEMENTS HISTORY

ABSORB

{also use in Accountability, Attention to Detail, Cognitive Load Management, Commitment and Dedication, Common Sense, Cross-Cultural Competency, Flexibility, Learn, and Self-Manageable}

(1) become captivated, fascinated, engaged, interested, or preoccupied in; fascinate

(1) The strategic planning process <u>absorbed</u> much of my time.

(2) draw into oneself; grasp; grip; realize; recognize; take in; understand

(3) acquire; assimilate; attract; consume; digest; endure; engulf; imbibe; soak up; sustain; take in; take up; use up

Résumé bullet points:

- <u>Absorbed</u> additional new department, including personnel, budget, and objectives, and led all managers in department productivity gains of prior year

ACCELERATE

{also use in Commitment and Dedication, Self-Manageable, Motivated, and Time and Organizational Management}

(1) gather speed; go faster; grow; hurry; increase speed of; pick up the pace; quicken; rush speed up

(2) cause to occur sooner

<u>Collocates to: change, depreciation, development, process, program, place, time, trend</u>

Résumé bullet points:

- <u>Accelerated</u> the process of new hire to fully trained status by 20 percent without any loss in efficiency

ACCLAIM

{also use in Self-Confident and Social Intelligence}

(1)   acknowledge or declare approval; applaud; cheer; commend; hail; praise vociferously; sing one's praises

(1) Steve Jobs was widely <u>acclaimed</u> as a visionary.

<u>Collocates to: actor, author, critic, entertainer, film, hero, inventor, movie, musician, public, television, writer</u>

Résumé bullet points:

- <u>Acclaimed</u> by industry trade press to have developed the most innovative training process in the industry, enabling new hires to achieve certification status in half the time of the industry standard

ACCOMMODATE

{also use in Common Sense, Compassion, Cross-Cultural Competency, Customer Awareness, and Outgoing}

(1)   house; lodge; provide accommodations; put up

(2)   adapt; be big enough for; contain; have capacity for; hold; reconcile; seat

(3)   do a favor or a service for someone; oblige

(4)   acclimate; acclimatize; adjust; become accustomed; familiarize; get used to; make fit or suitable for

(5)   allow for; assist; be of service; consider; find ways to help; oblige
<u>Collocates to: change, demand, desire, difference, growth, guest, need, passengers, request, schedule, space, special case(s), student</u>

ACCOMPLISH

{also use in Accountability, Accuracy and Precision, Attention to Detail, Drive, Leadership, Motivated, Novel and Adaptive Thinking, Passion and Tenacity, and Work Ethic}

(1)   achieve; attain; bring about; carry out; cause to happen; complete; do; finish; gain; get done; finish; fulfill; make happen; make possible; produce; pull off; reach; realize; undertake
<u>Collocates to: aim, feats, goals, learning, luminary, mission, objectives, purpose, tasks</u>

Résumé bullet points:

- <u>Accomplished </u>record for new sales increasing new accounts by 25% over prior year

ACCUMLATE

(1)   accrue; add; amass; build up; collect; gather; hoard

(2)   accrete; grow larger by adding; mount up
<u>Collocates to: assets, data, debt, evidence, information, influence, knowledge, power, money, wealth</u>

ACHIEVE

{also use in Attitude, Drive and Passion, Education, Leadership, Motivated, Novel and Adaptive Thinking, Risk Tolerant, and Self-Confident}

(1)   accomplish; attain; complete; conclude; do; finish; get; perform; pull off; reach; realize

(2)   succeed in doing something
<u>Collocates to: balance, fame, goals, honor, objectives, outcome, reputation, results, success</u>

Résumé bullet points:

- <u>Achieved</u> the status of Fellow

ACQUIRE

{also use in Customer Awareness, Design Mind-Set, Gather Data and Convert into Information, and Risk Tolerant}

(1)   attained; buy; come to possess; earn; gain; get; hold; obtain; purchase; receive
Résumé bullet points:

- <u>Acquired</u> the highest IEEE certification in 2012

ACTIVATE

{also use in Commitment and Dedication, Critical Thinking and Problem Solving, HARD SKILLS: Time and Organizational Management, and Novel and Adaptive Thinking}

(1)   acetify; become active; energize; galvanize; get going; initiate; make active; set in motion; set off; start; stimulate; trigger; turn off
Résumé bullet points:

- <u>Activated</u> the budget contingency for the project and delivered the results on schedule

ACTUALIZE

{also use in Attention to Detail, Common Sense, Motivated, and Novel and Adaptive Thinking}

(1) make real or actual; make something actual or real; realize; represent or describe realistically

(2) fulfill the potential of

Collocates to: act, communion, desire, ideal, goal, potential, virtue

Résumé bullet points:

- Actualized virtual transactions, giving customers a human contact

ACTUATE

{also use in Attention to Detail, Accuracy, Creativity, Customer Awareness, Leadership, and Risk Tolerant}

(1) activate; arouse to action; give incentive for action; motivate; move to act; put into motion; start; trigger

Collocates to: application, breaks, desire, device, drive, motion, plan, program, shock

ADAPT

{also use in Attention to Detail, Commitment and Dedication, Common Sense, Creativity, Cross-Cultural Competency, Flexibility, HARD SKILLS: Engineering and R&D, and Learn}

(1) acclimate; accommodate; adjust; change; conform; fashion; fit; get used to; make suitable; reconcile; square; suit; tailor

(2) make fit, often by modification

(3) cause something to change for the better

Résumé bullet points:

- Adapted innovative database approaches and identified two new untapped market segments that added 10 percent profits in 2 years

ADD

(1) add up; adjoin; affix; append; attach; combine; count up; include; insert; put in; tally; total; tote up

(2) augment; complement; enhance; enlarge; improve; increase; intensify; supplement; swell

ADDUCE

(1)   allege; bring forward; cite as evidence; lead to; present; provide advance evidence for something; put forward

(1)   "Whoever in discussion <u>adduces</u> authority uses not intellect but memory."

—Leonardo da Vinci

<u>Collocates to: argument, authority, case, concept, data, development, evidence, example, reason, term, theory</u>

ADOPT

{also use in Accountability and Commitment and Dedication}

(1)   accept; agree to; approve; assume; embrace; endorse; espouse; foster; implement; take in as one's own; talk on; take up; take on board

Résumé bullet points:

   • <u>Adopted</u> the ISO standards for Environmental Management System (EMS)

ADVANCE

{also use in Self-Manageable}

(1)   continue; evolve; forward; further; go ahead; go forward; proceed; increase; move ahead; move forward; move on; press forward; press on; proceed; progress

(2)   build up; develop; enhance; expand; promote; rise; spread

Résumé bullet points:

   • <u>Advanced</u> a more rigorous standard for customer service representatives

AFFECT

(1)   act physically on something or someone; change; concern; connect closely and often indiscriminately; have an effect on; have an emotional or cognitive impact on; impinge on; impress; influence; move; shape; strike; sway; touch

(2)   distress; disturb; move; touch; upset

(3)   assume; fake; imitate; pretend or have; put on

<u>Collocates to: ability, behavior, change, community, condition, decisions, factor, health, issue, level, life, performance, policy, quality</u>

Résumé bullet points:

- <u>Affected</u> the more adopted timely approach for resolving customer complaints by showing employees videos of the actual impact of customer service failures

AMALGAMATE

(1)   combine; fuse; integrate; join together; merge; mix; unite

AMASS

{also use in Drive and Passion, Education, Motivated, and Self-Manageable}

(1)   accrue; accumulate; assemble; build up; collect; compile; gather together; hoard; pile up; store up

Résumé bullet points:

- <u>Amassed</u> 75 customer appreciation letters and recommendations

AMELIORATE

{also use with Accountability. Accuracy and Preciseness, Attention to Detail, Creativity, Leadership, Learn, Novel and Adaptive Thinking, and Self-Manageable}

(1)   amend; correct a mistake; enhance; enrich; get better; improve; make better; perfect; tolerate; upgrade

(2)   correct a deficiency or defect; make right a wrong; take action that makes up for one's negative or improper actions

<u>Collocates to: concern, condition, consequences, distress, effect, effort, pain, plan, problem, situation, stress, symptom, system, tension</u>

ASCERTAIN

(1)   determine; discover; establish; find out; learn; realize; uncover

(2)   find out with certainty

ASSEMBLE

(1)   accumulate; combine; convene; group; mass produce; produce standardized goods in large volumes; unite

ATTAIN

{also use in Education}

(1)   accomplish; acquire; achieve; arrive at; conquer; gain; make; manage; obtain; procure; reach; realize

Résumé bullet points:

- <u>Attained</u> the highest level of certification awarded by the IEEE

AUTHOR

{also use in Communications and Creativity}

(1)   create; pen; scribe; source; write

(1) "He who purposes to be an <u>author</u> should first be a student."

—Dryden

Résumé bullet points:

- <u>Authored</u> the company's diversity engagement strategy which received national acclaim for the firm

AVAIL

(1)   be of advantage, help, take; use to one's advantage to accomplish an end
<u>Collocates to: benefit, freedom, language, opportunity, option, privilege, protection, resource, service, tool</u>

BEGET

(1)   cause something; create something; father; lead to; procreate; reproduce

BEGUILE

(1)   attract; charm into doing; deceive; divert; enthrall; entice; fascinate; influence by slyness; lure; mesmerize; put under a spell; sawder; woo

(1) "I am not merry; but I do <u>beguile</u> the thing I am, by seeming otherwise."

—William Shakespeare

(2) "If the weak hand, that has recorded this tale, has, by its scenes, <u>beguiled</u> the mourner of one hour of sorrow, or, by its moral, taught him to sustain it—the effort, however humble, has not been vain, nor is the writer unrewarded."

—Ann Radcliffe

<u>Collocates to: audience, composition, view</u>

BOOST

(1)   advance; amplify; augment; enhance; further; heighten; hoist; improve; increase; lift; make better; raise

(1) Tim's new idea <u>boosted</u> sales in the market by 20 percent.

CATAPULT

(1) throw or force something

(2) advance quickly over peers; leap frog or jump obstacles or barriers

CIRCUMNAVIGATE

(1) go around but not through; pass; get around something by intelligence, nerve, guile, luck or determination; skirt

COADJUTE

(1) cooperate; work together

COALESCE

{also use in Accountability, Cognitive Load Management, Commitment and Dedication, Cross-Cultural Competency, Flexibility, Leadership, Learn, Social Intelligence, and Team Player}

(1) blend; combine; come together as one; fuse or cause to grow together; join; merge; mingle; mix together different elements or parts; unite
<u>Collocates to: beliefs, filter, ideas, image, matter, movement, shapes, opposition, views</u>

COLLABORATE

{also use in Commitment and Dedication, Communication, Cross-Cultural Competency, Self-Manageable, Take Direction, and Work Ethic}

(1) act as a team; assist; cooperate; pool resources; team up; work together on a common enterprise or project; work jointly with

(1) Dawn successfully <u>collaborated</u> with two other agencies.

(2) cooperate as a traitor; quisling
Résumé bullet points:

> • <u>Collaborated</u> with local universities to develop hands-on industrial training programs as extensions to classroom learning

COLLATE

(1) arrange; assemble; catalog; check; classify; codify; compare critically; gather; order; organize; set up
<u>Collocates to: data, information, numbers, record, results, report, study, survey</u>

Résumé bullet points:

- Collated 75 years of consumer records into firm's first searchable database

COMMUNICATE

(1)   be in touch; commune; connect; converse; convey something; correspond; exchange a few words; share; transfer; write

COMPLETE

{also use in Accountability, Commitment and Dedication, Education, Self-Manageable, and Work Ethic}

(1)   be done; choate; conclude; entire; finish a task; integral; perfect; through; unabridged; uncut; whole; wrap up

Résumé bullet points:

- Completed the industry's top certification in less time than anyone at the firm

COMPORT

(1)   act; agree; behave in a certain, proper way

COMPOSE

(1)   collect; contain; control; cool down; practice; restrain; settle; simmer down

(2)   create; incite; produce; write

CONCEIVE

{also use in Accountability, Critical Thinking and Problem Solving, and Self-Management}

(1)   create; envisage; imagine; invent original idea; picture; visualize

   (1) I conceived and wrote the firm's long term strategic plan.

(2)   begin life; dream; elaborate; form; make up

CONTROL

{also use in Self-Manageable and HARD SKILLS: Administrative and Organizational}

(1)   be in charge of; be in command; direct; dominate; govern; have influence or power over; manage; organize; oversee; rule; run

COORDINATE

{also use in Attention to Detail, Critical Thinking and Problem Solving, and Self-Manageable}

Résumé bullet point:

- Coordinated $20 million sales and marketing budget for gaming division of global firm

CREATE

{also use in Creativity}

Résumé bullet points:

- Created a spreadsheet report process that improved productivity and reduced division costs by $200,000

DEFINE

{also use with Accountability, Accuracy and Preciseness, Attention to Detail, Critical Thinking and Problem Solving, and Design Mind-Set}

DESIGN

{also use in Creativity and HARD SKILLS: Computer Literate, Engineering, and Research}

(1)   aim; contrive; devise; intend; make designs; mean; plan; propose; set apart for some purpose

(2)   conceive; construct; create; draw up blueprints or plans; fabricate; invent; originate

(3)   blueprint; cast; chart; draw up; frame; map; project; set out

Résumé bullet points:

- Designed a tracking system that allowed service repairman and their vehicles to be routed to jobs by an algorithm based on geographic and priority

DEVELOP

{also use in Self-Manageable}

(1)   achieve; advance; build up; evolve; expand; exploit; expound; extend; gain; generate; grow; increase; mature; strengthen; unfold; widen

(2)   make known gradually

Résumé bullet points:

- Developed and maintained documentation and communications for two worldwide projects

DEVISE

{also use in Creativity and HARD SKILLS: Engineering and R&D}

Résumé bullet point:

- <u>Devised</u> the solution for more efficient routing of service trucks, saving thousands of dollars of fuel and making service calls more efficient. Developed algorithm that calculated new emergency calls, distance from current call, and estimated time of service

DIRECT

(1)   conduct; command; lead; take action immediately

(2)   control the course; guide; point the way; show the way

Résumé bullet points:

- <u>Directed</u> the firm's diversity awareness program

- <u>Directed</u> in-house sales training classes

DISCOVER

{also use in Common Sense, Intelligence, Critical Thinking and Problem Solving, Gather Data and Convert into Information}

(1)   ascertain; be first to learn something; determine; expose; find out; hear; learn; realize, see, or uncover something

Résumé bullet points:

- <u>Discovered</u> new market for industrial waste creating a new revenue channel of $100,000 annually

DISTRIBUTE

(1)   apportion; arrange; deal; dispense; divide; divvy; dole out; measure; parcel; portion; scatter; share; spread

Résumé bullet points:

- <u>Distributed</u> surplus material from production to sheltered workshops in the area providing hundreds of handicapped workers with continued employment

DOUBLE

(1)   duplicate; improve or grow something twice its previous level or size

Résumé bullet points:

- <u>Doubled</u> customer retention rates increasing profits by $800,0000

DRIVE

(1)   force; guide; herd; impel; make; motor; plunge; pilot; propel; push; ram; run; shove; steer; thrust; wheel

EARN

{also use in Education}

(1)   acquire as a result of one's behavior or effort; draw down; gain; make; merit; pull down; receive; receive wages; win; work for

(2)   receive salary, commission, pay, or rent for one's effort

(3)   gain interest as profit

Résumé bullet points:

- Earned an MBA and CPA in less than three years while working full time

ENHANCE

{also use in Leadership and Motivated}

(1)   add to; augment; boost; develop; endow with beauty and elegance; grace

(2)   improve the quality or condition of

(3)   digitally or electronically improve the quality, tone, pitch, image of photos, recordings, images

Résumé bullet points:

- Enhanced key account cross-selling activities by 17 percent in one year using multidiscipline team approach to customer renewal project

ESTABLISH

{also use in Accountability, Reliability, and Self-Confidence}

(1)   begin; create; enact; ensconce; found; install; institute; prove; set up; settle; start

(2)   make firm; make stable

(3)   bring about; cause to happen

(4)   settle in an office or position

(5)   cause to accept or recognize; set up permanently

(6)   demonstrate; prove

Résumé bullet points:

- Established first company job share policy allowing firm to keep more experienced workers and hire additional talented candidates

EXCEED

{also use in Accountability and Drive, Passion, and Tenacity}

(1) be more or greater than; beat; go beyond; surpass what was expected or thought possible; outdo

Résumé bullet points:

• Exceeded all company records for reduction of loss prevention, reducing losses as percent of sales by 30 percent in one year

EXPAND

(1) enlarge; increase; inflate; swell

(2) open up; spread out; stretch out; unfold

(3) dilate; enlarge; extend; make greater in size, bulk, or scope

(4) work out or show the full form of

Résumé bullet points:

• Expanded the conversion rate of leads by 75 percent in 2 years, increasing the number of new sales by 40 percent

EXPEDIT

{also use in Drive and Passion and Time Management}

(1) accelerate; hurry up; rush

(2) speed up or make easy the process or action of

(3) dispatch; issue officially; send off

Résumé bullet points:

• Expedited the acceptance pace of new policy applications by 50 percent by adding automated policy holder data from firm's data warehouse

FIX

{also use in Accomplishments and Achievements and Critical Thinking}

(1) affix; arrange; assign; attach; blame; fasten; impute; pin on; place saddle; produce deep impression; secure

(2) engrave

(3) mend; replace; restore

Résumé bullet points:

• Fixed and repaired many old pieces of production equipment still functional, saving hundreds of thousands of dollars in capital costs

FOUND

(1)   begin; constitute; create; establish; institute; organize; set up; start
Résumé bullet points:

   • <u>Founded</u> the firm's first employee social capital training program

FULFILL

{also use in Accountability and Reliability}

(1)   carry out; complete an assignment; discharge; execute; exercise; imple-
      ment; perform; satisfy
Résumé bullet points:

   • <u>Fulfilled</u> the requirements for certification, becoming the first employee
      from the company to be recognized by the Project Management Institute

FURTHER

(1)   additional; advance; back; give aid; go beyond; support; promote
Résumé bullet points:

   • <u>Furthered</u> my education by volunteering to work the graveyard shift so I
      could attend morning classes at a nearby university

GUIDE

{also use in Accountability}

(1)   channel; conduct; direct; funnel; point

(2)   escort; lead; pilot; route; show; steer; supervise; surround; usher
Résumé bullet points:

   • <u>Guided</u> the project management team tasked with rebranding the
      75-year-old flagship brand; succeed in re-launching with a 10% gain in
      market share

HELP

{also use in Companionate and Polite}

(1)   abet; aid; assist; benefit; change for the better; improve; succor
Résumé bullet points:

   • <u>Helped</u> strategic planning committee draft the firm's new mission
      statement

IMPACT

(1)   affect

(1) My business plan <u>impacted</u> the investment club by creating a great deal of positive publicity.

(2)   fix firmly; forcefully wedge; make contact, especially force tightly together

Résumé bullet points:

- <u>Impacted</u> positive consumer reaction to the firm's new market entry by heavy use of celebrity endorsements and the mass media

IMPLEMENT

{also use in Accountability and HARD SKILLS: Administrative and Organizational}

(1)   accomplish; apply; carry out; complete; effect; employ; enforce; execute; fulfill; finish; instigate; put into action; put into operation; put into place; put into practice; put into service; realize; use

Résumé bullet points:

- <u>Implemented</u> first social media marketing campaign improving brand awareness by 30%

IMPROVE

{also use in Accountability and HARD SKILLS: Research and R&D}

(1)   ameliorate; amend; better; build up; develop; employ; enhance in value; enrich; expand; further; get better; help; increase; make better; meliorate; perfect; raise to a better quality; upgrade use

(2)   convalesce; get better; get stronger; get well; make progress; mend; perk up; rally; recover

Résumé bullet points:

- <u>Improved</u> customer cross sales by over $250,000 in first year of program

INITIATE

{also use in Critical Thinking and Self-Manageable}

(1)   begin; commence; create; inaugurate; induct; install; instate; instigate; introduce; invest; kick off; open; set off; start

(2)   coach; instruct; mentor; teach; train; tutor

Résumé bullet points:

- <u>Initiated</u> customer retention, renewal, and referral program which resulted in an increase in renewals and referred sales leading to a growth in profits of $600,000

LEAD

(1) be first; captain; command; conduct; control; direct the operations, activity, or performance; escort; go ahead; go in front; guide on a way especially by going in advance; head; manage; officer; pilot; show the way

Résumé bullet points:

- <u>Led</u> all 500 salespeople in the firm in new sales for five consecutive years (2007-2011)

MAKE

{also use in Engineering and R&D}

(1) assemble; become; build; cause; compose; construct; create; develop; do; enact; erect; execute; fabricate; fashion; forge; form; frame; manufacture; mold; prepare; produce; put together; require; shape

Résumé bullet points:

- <u>Made</u> 20% more prototypes in the same time frame than any department

MANAGE

{also use in Administrative, Organization, and Planning, and HARD SKILLS: Business and Business Sense}

(1) administer; be in charge of; conduct or direct affairs; oversee; regulate; run; supervise

(2) do; fare; fend; get along; get by; make do; muddle through

(3) control the behavior of; handle; succeed in dealing with

(4) succeed despite difficulties

Résumé bullet points:

- <u>Managed</u> a department with a budget of $22 million

MARSHAL

(1) arrange; assemble; gather all resources to achieve a goal; mobilize; organize

(2) put in delineated order

MAXIMIZE

{also use in Accomplishments and Achievements, Accountability, Drive, and Passion and Tenacity}

(1)   make best use of; make as great or as large as possible; raise to the highest possible degree

Résumé bullet points

- Maximized the annual bonus opportunity for sales people by June four years in row (2008-2012)

ORGANIZE

(1)   arrange systematically; categorize; make arrangements, plans, or preparations for; order; put in order; sort out; systematize

(2)   control; coordinate; fix; manage; take charge

Résumé bullet points:

- Organized the annual company 3-day sales meeting and training seminar for 300 attendees

ORIGINATE

(1)   bring into being; create or initiate; have a specified beginning; initiate; invent; make; start off

(2)   begin; come from; derive; start; stem from

Résumé bullet points

- Originated the "money back membership guarantee" for association memberships which increased memberships with no negative financial backlash

PIONEER

{also use in Creativity, Drive, Passion and Tenacity, Motivated, Self-Confidence, and Self-Manageable}

(1)   be the first to develop new ideas or concepts; lead the way

Résumé bullet points

- Pioneered free trials in an expendable product field resulting in 10-13% growth rates over five years

PRODUCE

(1)   achieve; accomplish; finish a task

(2)   bring forth; produce; yield

Résumé bullet points

- • <u>Produced</u> the largest increase in personal sales over the prior year in company history, 280% (2011–2012)

QUARTERBACK

(1)   direct; lead; manage

RECRUIT

(1)   bring in; hire for specific skills, abilities, and capabilities; seek out over others

Résumé bullet points:

- • <u>Recruited</u> to turn around unprofitable, unproductive, inefficient division

RECTIFY

{also use in SOFT SKILLS: Accountability and HARD SKILLS: Accounting and Finance}

(1)   amend; correct; fix; put right; resolve; set right

(2)   adjust; cure; remedy; repair; mend

(3)   convert

SECURE

(1)   fasten; fix securely; hold; lock; make safe

(2)   acquire; get hands on; get hold of; obtain

SELECT

(1)   choose; pick; vote

(2)   chose one in preference over another; pick out one based on some quality of excellence

(3)   limit to certain groups based on some standard

Résumé bullet points:

- • <u>Selected</u> to lead corporate team tasked with applying for the JD Powers award for customer satisfaction

- • <u>Selected</u> to create and develop firm's exhibit and presence at global logistics conference and exhibit, Hamburg, Germany 2012

SOLVE

{also use in Creativity, Design Mind-Set, and Accounting and Finance}

(1)   find a solution; settle

(2)   provide or find a suitable answer to a problem
Résumé bullet points:

- <u>Solved</u> numerous marketing problems by serving as inside consultant willing to look at issues with unbiased point of view

SPEARHEAD

{also use in Professional Demeanor and Risk Tolerance}

(1)   be in front of something; point; take the lead
Résumé bullet points:

- <u>Spearheaded</u> the firm's strategic redeployment into recycling of Freon gases

TRANSFORM

(1)   change from one form to another; remake; renew; upgrade

(2)   change the personality or character of one

(3)   change the condition, nature, or function of
Résumé bullet points:

- <u>Transformed</u> out of date, demoralized, logistics operation into a state of the art career maker

WIN

(1)   claim victory; succeed
Résumé bullet points:

- <u>Won</u> the Industry's Star Performer award three years (2009-2011)

EDUCATION AND TRAINING, DEGREES, AND CERTIFICATIONS

ACHIEVE

{also use in Achievements and Accomplishments, Attitude, Drive and Passion, Leadership, Motivated, Novel and Adaptive Thinking, Risk Tolerant, and Self-Confident}

(1)   accomplish; attain; complete; conclude; do; finish; get; perform; pull off; reach; realize

(2)   succeed in doing something
Résumé bullet points:

   • Achieved the highest industry certification possible

AMASS

{also use in Accomplishments and Achievements, Drive and Passion, Motivated, and Self-Manageable}

(1)   accrue; accumulate; assemble; build up; collect; compile; gather together; hoard; pile up; store up
Résumé bullet points:

   • Amassed 75 customer appreciation letters and recommendations

ATTAIN

{also use in Accomplishments and Achievements}

(1)   accomplish; achieve; acquire; arrive at; conquer; gain; make; manage; obtain; procure; reach; realize
Résumé bullet points:

   • Attained the industry's highest certification

COMPLETE

{also use in Accomplishments and Achievements, Accountability, Commitment and Dedication, Self-Manageable, and Work Ethic}

(1)   be done; choate; conclude; entire; finish a task; integral; perfect; through; unabridged; uncut; whole; wrap up
Résumé bullet points:

   • Completed four-year training and apprenticeship in plumbing and pipefitting at ABC Technical and Vocational School

EARN

{also use in Accomplishment and Achievements}

(1)   acquire as a result of one's behavior or effort; draw down; gain; make; merit; pull down; receive; wages; win; work for

(2)   receive salary, commission, pay, or rent for one's effort

(3)   gain interest as profit
Résumé bullet points:

   • Earned profit in first year after taking over failing division

GRADUATE

(1)   achieve passing grades in a course, training, or skill development

(2)   advance by proficiency, skill, or achievement; mark in degrees of measurement

Résumé bullet points:

- Graduated with an MBA having gone to school while continuing to work full time

HONOR

(1)   acclaim; admire; celebrate; distinguish; exalt; extol; glorify; hail; laud; magnify; panegyrize; praise someone or something for going beyond normal responsibilities; venerate

Résumé bullet points:

- Honored by Industry Trade Association for innovative ideas to grow business

LAUD

(1)   acclaim; applaud; celebrate; extol; mention; praise; speak well of

RECERTIFY

(1)   certify again; meet the standards; qualify again

(2)   declare something true, accurate, or certain

Sources

American Heritage. *400 Words You Should Know.* New York: Houghton Mifflin Harcourt Publishing Co., 2010.

Barker, John, and Kim Kellen. *Career Planning: A Development Approach.* Upper Saddle River, NJ: Merrill, 1998.

Beyer, Thomas, Jr., Ph.D. *501 English Verbs,* 2nd Edition. New York: Baron's Educational Series, 2007.

Bly, Robert. *The Words You Should Know to Sound Smart.* Avon, MA: Adams Media, 2009.

Dictionary by Hampton. application on iPhone.

Fenell, Barabara, A. *A History of the English.* Oxford, England: Blackwell Publishers, 2001.

Lucas, Stephen. *The Art of Public Speaking*, 9th Edition. Boston: McGraw Hill, 1983.

Montefiore, Simon Sebag. *Speeches That Changed the World.* London: Quercus Publishing, 2005.

Roget's II's The New Thesaurus. Editors, The America Heritage Dictionary. Boston: Houghton Mifflin Co., 1980.

Sisson, A.R. *Sisson's Word and Expression Locator.* West Nyak, NY: Parker Publishing Co., 1979.

www.writeexpress.com/action-verbs.html. Accessed August 2 through August 12, 2010.

www.rfp-templates.com/List-of-Action-Verbs.html. Accessed August 2 through August 12, 2010.

Index

*Words in **bold** are power verbs.

A

abduce, 55
aberrate, 113
abet, 5, 68, 158, 163, 200
abide, 5, 63, 68, 113, 178, 181, 191, 213
abound, 40, 181
abreach, 34
abreact, 75, 188
absorb, 6, 40, 55, 63, 68, 113, 141, 158, 192, 245
absterge, 29, 41
abstract, 56, 147
aby, 178, 181
accede, 6, 68, 123, 142, 173, 200, 205
accelerate, 69, 163, 192, 211, 220, 245
accentuate, 6, 29, 41, 56, 69, 75, 93, 135
accept, 7, 113, 181, 206, 208
accessorize, 38
acclaim, 188, 200, 246
acclimate, 41, 56, 63, 114, 142, 149, 159, 171, 178, 208, 213
acclimatize, 159
accommodate, 63, 89, 114, 123, 142, 173, 246
accomplish, 7, 29, 41, 135, 150, 163, 171, 213, 246
accomplishments. *See* achievements
accord, 175, 200
account for, 33, 42, 227, 231
accountability verbs, 5-29
accounting and finance verbs, 217-220
accredit, 7, 42, 181, 221
accredite, 123
accrue, 100, 192
accumlate, 247
accuracy verbs, 29-33, 40-55
accustom, 143
achieve, 34, 135, 150, 163, 171, 185, 188, 247, 263
achievements
    finding in book, 2
    in résumés, 2
    verbs, 245-263
acknowledge, 8, 145, 159, 173, 178, 192
acquaint, 114, 200
acquiesce, 8, 35, 56, 89, 201

acquire, 123, 125, 186, 242, 247
act, 150, 193
act on, 42, 221
activate, 69, 100, 171, 221, 247
actualize, 42, 64, 150, 164, 172, 248
actuate, 43, 93, 124, 151, 186, 248
adapt, 35, 43, 64, 69, 94, 114, 143, 159, 238, 248
adaptive thinking verbs, 171-173
add, 126, 248
address, 43, 76, 193
adduce, 8, 76, 151, 249
adhere, 100, 126
adjudicate, 9, 57, 101, 126
adjure, 76, 206
adjust, 9, 64, 115, 143, 214, 217
administer, 9, 182, 193, 217, 221
administrative verbs, 220-225
admire, 201
adopt, 10, 70, 249
adorn, 38
adumbrate, 57, 151, 186
advance, 193, 249
advertise, 76
advertising verbs, 225-227
advise, 89
advocate, 70, 90, 182, 188, 193
affect, 249
affirm, 10, 43, 101, 145
aggregate, 118, 201, 221
agree, 10, 143, 175
aid, 10, 115
alert, 193
align, 44, 70, 126, 194, 201
allay, 90, 115
alleviate, 90
allocate, 118
allude, 57, 76
ally, 115, 174, 201
alter, 11
alternate, 144
amalgamate, 250
amass, 136, 164, 194, 250, 264
ameliorate, 11, 30, 44, 94, 151, 160, 172, 194, 250

B

G–H

I

J–K–L

FINANCIAL TIMES

In an increasingly competitive world, it is quality
of thinking that gives an edge—an idea that opens new
doors, a technique that solves a problem, or an insight
that simply helps make sense of it all.

We work with leading authors in the various arenas
of business and finance to bring cutting-edge thinking
and best-learning practices to a global market.

It is our goal to create world-class print publications
and electronic products that give readers
knowledge and understanding that can then be
applied, whether studying or at work.

To find out more about our business
products, you can visit us at www.ftpress.com.